THE
Rainbow
Witch

THE
Rainbow Witch

ENHANCE YOUR MAGIC WITH
THE SECRET POWERS OF COLOR

KAC YOUNG, PhD

STERLING ETHOS
New York

STERLING ETHOS
New York

STERLING ETHOS and the distinctive Sterling Ethos logo
are registered trademarks of Sterling Publishing Co., Inc.

Text © 2023 Kac Young

ISBN 978-1-4549-4983-1
ISBN 978-1-4549-4984-8 (e-book)

Library of Congress Control Number: 2023944500

For information about custom editions, special sales, and premium purchases,
please contact specialsales@unionsquareandco.com.

Printed in India

2 4 6 8 10 9 7 5 3 1

unionsquareandco.com

Cover and interior design by Jo Obarowski
Cover images by Shutterstock.com: Victoria Bat; Kovalov Anatolii (background)

Image credits appear on pages 215–216

Dedicated with eternal love
to the amazing, talented,
funny, brilliant, inspiring,
and fabulous
Marlene Morris.

Thank you for twenty
glorious years.

CONTENTS

INTRODUCTION:
IN PRAISE OF THE RAINBOW

There is more to color than meets the eye, although we see color everywhere. It's so uniquely powerful that even a color-blind person can still sense and feel it. Certain colors can impact our emotions, our moods, and sometimes, even our behaviors. Under certain circumstances it can be a source of information, like a traffic light regulating the flow of traffic. Color is a very personal experience, and yet often those personal experiences speak to what we have in common with others, which gives us a shared understanding of the meaning of each color.

This shared understanding is the focus of scientists, psychologists, and marketers who all wish to channel its effects. But it is the metaphysical effect of the rainbow that we are going to learn to channel in this book, not as clinicians but as students and fans of the colors of the rainbow. This is a book about becoming a Rainbow Witch, who focuses their practice on color power and how it can be turned into magic.

One of the most spectacular of natural displays is the rainbow: its bold colors, gleaming in the sunlight, form a bridge between the cosmos and earth. It's a breathtaking sight. In this book, we are going to investigate the rainbow and describe the qualities, characteristics, and power of each of its seven primary colors. We will learn how to use those colors in spells and meditations, for cleaning chakras, and as tools for creating new outcomes. In essence, we will be putting color to use for you and your loved ones, as well as using each ray of the rainbow for personal and metaphysical power.

We'll take you through compatible symbols, archetypes, oils, herbs, plants, deities, planets, days of the week, and more. Acquainted with these characteristics, you'll be the smartest witch on your block and able to use what we present you for heightened power and efficacy in your work. If you're not already a practicing witch, you can begin here and learn these magical rays and ways. This book does not tell you exactly what to do: it honors your intuition and imagination for utilizing what is presented in these pages. Consider this a book of information and inspiration to help you increase your power using the colors of the rainbow.

I'll tell you what I know, add to that what you know, and then provide you room to take flight. If something doesn't appeal to you, don't use it. Let's say you've never used magical birds in your practice before. I encourage you to experiment with their energies and see how they broaden your reach and open your connections to other worlds. If you haven't been introduced to making and using sigils, stand by for a fantastic experience. Sigils are powerful symbols that you create based on your desires and dreams. They work like a charm and can make a huge difference in your life and practice. The same goes for crystals and essential oils. Seek information if you need to learn more about each discipline. There are charts and references in the back of the book to help you with some of the esoteric meanings behind what we present.

I speak as though you're already a witch, because if you picked up this book, something in you already is. Choosing the path of the Rainbow Witch is a positive affirmation of life itself and will deepen who you are, add meaning to your days, and bring you into a community of extraordinary and powerful practitioners and white witches. I can't wait for you to be part of this clan, to learn what we have to offer, and to invite you to experience the initiations into each color that will lift you to greater heights of understanding, love, and compassion for yourself and others.

You will need a few things as we go along. A journal for each of the colors of the rainbow will help provide a perfect space for you to record your impressions as you read through each chapter: red, orange, yellow, green, blue, indigo, and violet. I also recommend using matching pens in the ink color of the ray. Living that color by wearing it on your body and decorating yourself with it as you study can also be a fantastic tool in aligning yourself with its energy. Perhaps a set of scarves in the seven colors, or hats . . . anything to mark the significance of the ray we are working with.

Each initiation to the rays includes a process for you to follow. Please don't rush through these initiations. They are designed for your spiritual growth and progression up the ladder of colors so you can truly master their potency. Make it fun, kind of like a party, and you will get the most benefits out of this book and the initiations. You can always go back and revisit any of them if something occurs that gets you off track for a bit. Recenter yourself at any time and rekindle the power of the colors.

THE RAINBOW BLESSING

All hail the glorious rainbow,

Given to us from the divine grace of the Universe,

Placed in our realm to enjoy and utilize.

Let us use the power it holds

For good in the world,

For good in our lives,

And to empower all of our thoughts and actions

As sent forth from our hearts and hands.

Let us be hereafter filled with love,

Overflowing gratitude for the blessings

Of the seven color sisters our beloved rainbow shines.

All hail. All praise, All love and Blessed Be.

WHO IS A RAINBOW WITCH?

A Rainbow Witch is the bodhisattva of all witches. They are people who see the good in everyone and every living thing. They embrace all colors, shapes, textures, and beliefs, and understand that everything and everyone alive is pure energy. When Carl Sagan said, "we are all star stuff," he was talking about energy. The Rainbow Witch works with universal energy on the mundane planes to heal, connect, purify, consecrate, and transform themselves and their lives into what they choose it to be. They are never at the behest of experience; they are the co-creators of it. This gives them the power to live life in joy all the time, because they possess the power to create it.

Rainbow Witches practice kindness and are in tune with the world, as well as being united with the cosmos. The ultimate power of the Rainbow Witch is that they can bring any practice from any other religion or belief system, or from any other witchcraft discipline, and use the extra power of the seven rainbow colors to expand and enhance their work.

Some Rainbow Witches prefer to work with angels, faeries, gods, goddesses, crystals, animals, herbs, and many other things. When they add the power and vibration of color to their work and spells, they invoke an entirely new blend of power.

A Rainbow Witch is a gathering hearth for all witches. Think of this practice as the umbrella under which all magic workers can stand and benefit from the rays of the rainbow and the magic contained within each color that makes up a rainbow. A Rainbow Witch isn't just one thing. They are prismatic witches centered in love, light, color, vibration, and freedom. And they put all of those to use simultaneously.

The Rainbow Witch also possesses ultimate freedom. They can practice rituals that attract and empower them. They can connect with the moon by honoring its eight phases and rising tides; they may understand the innate power of crystal energy and use stones and crystals to direct their intentions. They use candle magic when they choose, and often incorporate pendulums into their quests. Sometimes they might use divination tools like the runes, the Ogham, the I Ching, or the tarot for help solving certain problems and to answer questions they pose. They can connect with other realms for advice; and check in with angels or guides. A Rainbow Witch does not follow a particular curriculum. In fact, they usually are already witches who want to add a little spice to what they already know.

Let's introduce the colors and get to know their individual influences.

THE MEANING OF COLOR

Color is simply the way our brain interprets the different wavelengths of light. For humans to even see color, light must be present. Light travels through the universe in waves. When sunlight hits the light waves, it connects with the gases and particles in the earth's atmosphere that the light waves are traversing. The impact of that physical connection scatters the waves in all directions.

The sun's rays house all the colors of the rainbow mixed together. At the end of the day, as the sun approaches the horizon, the atmosphere is most dense. Hence, the blue waves scatter first, and the red and yellow waves get through strongly enough to create what our eyes perceive as a majestic sunset.

We know those seven colors are linked to many things in nature, and especially the physical world. For the Rainbow Witch, every color in the rainbow connects with its focus in the physical world and comes alive with special meaning that consecrates it to certain intentions, emotions, and spell power. Each color contains a unique vibration, which can be used for any magical activity. Using the color spectrum gives the Rainbow Witch more power than other witches because their actions and intentions are infused with the power and the vibration of each ray of color. Witches from other disciplines can utilize the colors of the rainbow to enhance their work, too. According to neo-Theosophical writer Alice Bailey, "When the Logos (the consciousness of the divine being, the Sun) uttered the great cosmic Word for this solar system, three major streams of color issued forth, breaking almost simultaneously into another four, so giving us the seven streams of color by which manifestation becomes possible." She is referring to the colors contained in the rainbow.

The Rainbow Witch has the gift of working with the seven rainbow colors, using their unique powers to cast their spells and draw enhanced power to their work. Each color provides a witch with an edge when it comes to a particular kind of magical power. When you become aware of the power of each color, you'll be able to employ the perfect one as you cast each spell or call upon the energies of the magic that you are turning toward.

THE SEVEN RAYS OF THE RAINBOW

To understand how to tap in to the power of the rainbow using each of its seven colors, let's have a quick overview of the meaning of the colors we will be discussing.

RED represents passion, pleasure, power, anger, action, vibrance, energy, love, and conquest. The color red also means beginnings and forward motion. It is fire and blood.

ORANGE is an inviting and joyous color. It suggests warmth, heat, sunshine, sociability, enthusiasm, creativity, success, encouragement, shift, transformation, intelligence, harmony, aspiration, determination, good health, and active stimulation. It is the signature color of the extrovert.

YELLOW is an impactful color because it calls attention to itself. In medieval times, yellow signaled bravery, loyalty, and honor, and for those reasons it is used in family crests and painted on shields. It also means self-worth, courage, and power. It signifies the sun, creativity, warmth, intellect, positivity, and most of all, clarity.

GREEN is the color of life on earth, nature, freshness, fertility as well as money, finances, banking, and participating in the cycles of harmonic balance. It signifies rebirth and regeneration, youth, adventure, sentimentality, and health. It also specifically represents how we all recover after a setback or devastation.

On the surface, **BLUE** may appear to be a simple energy, but don't let it fool you—the color blue has many layers. On one level it is a calming color, but it can also represent "the blues" and how one feels when they have lost a love and don't know where to turn. It is the color of the sky above us, open spaces, freedom, expansiveness, inspiration, and sensitivity.

The color **INDIGO** reflects the color of the depths of water and the nighttime sky, which symbolizes our connection to the cosmos and our journey to greater depths. Indigo is the color associated with the third eye chakra, the pineal gland, and intuition, which is connected to the element of water. It tells us that there is more to "see" than meets the eye and that the truth lies below the surface. It represents fluidity, strength, insight, expressiveness, and perception on several levels.

DEEP VIOLET is associated with royalty, power, and ambition. There is also a dedicated sense of humanitarianism combined with visionary and artistic pursuits. It stands for high ideals, devotion, peace, grandeur, spirituality, and fragility. However, the violet ray can also mean immaturity in the sense that one clings to an unrealistic ideal when it is clear that it is unfeasible.

DATE CORRESPONDENCES

What this means to the Rainbow Witch is that you can work your magical spells, ceremonies, and rituals at any time, but you can focus those powers and increase the potency of your magic using the extra power of certain color rays.

You may want to cast a spell at a specific time and on a specific day. Both the year and the days of the week are associated with particular colors. For example:

Certain rays are more powerful at certain times of the year. As the sun's potency changes throughout the year when the earth revolves around it, so too the colored ray energies are more concentrated at different times. Even though the seasons are different in the northern and southern hemispheres, the potency of the rays remains the same.

Red ray is Jan. 1–Feb. 21.

Orange ray is Feb. 22–Apr. 14

Yellow ray is Apr. 15–Jun. 5

Green ray is Jun. 6–Jul. 27

Blue ray is Jul. 8–Sep. 19

Indigo ray is Sep. 20–Nov. 9

Violet ray is Nov. 10–Dec. 31

There are certain days of the week that are more potent for each ray. Monday is red, Tuesday is orange, Wednesday is yellow, Thursday is green, Friday is blue, Saturday is indigo, and Sunday is violet.

It would be a good idea to combine your magic work with the rainbow color that can enhance it, to make it even more powerful. As you come to understand more about each ray of color, you will know which ray on which day will be best for your chosen spells. It will all depend on your intention and desired outcome.

For example, if a Rainbow Witch wanted to create a particularly powerful love spell, they might want to avoid casting it on a day of the week or time of the year associated with the blue ray. Instead, they would most likely want to choose dates aligned with the red and orange rays. So a love spell worked on a Monday during the period of January 1 through February 21 would produce the highest and most potent spell power, garnering you the most successful result.

METHODS TO CHANNEL EACH RAY

In each chapter, we'll discover a variety of methods that will help you channel the power of each ray. In the words of Alice Bailey, "When it is known by the occultist which color is applicable to which plane, and which color therefore is the basic hue for that plane, he has grasped the fundamental secret of microcosmic development, and can build his body of manifestation by means of the same laws that Logos employed in building His objective solar system." *Logos* is her word for "the consciousness of the

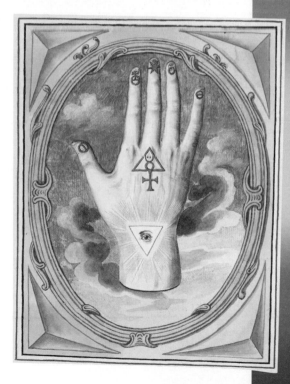

HOW TO CREATE YOUR OWN ALTAR

Location is important. Select a space where you can have privacy to practice your magic and spells. Most of all, use your intuition and you will easily locate the perfect area. Your feelings will be your best guide.

Size does not matter, but privacy does. Select something on which you can place your sacred items. Maybe even use an altar cloth. Some people like to have photos or mementoes of their ancestors, candles, crystals, flowers, symbols, feathers, writing paper, magic wish paper, icons, statues, sigils, symbols, cloths, books, journal, tarot and oracle cards, runes, Ogham, essential oils, seashells, rocks, bark, incense or a diffuser, or anything you treasure and hold in your heart.

Your altar is your temple, just as your body is. It is a place to be cherished and revered. It should be the go-to place for prayer work, chanting, psychic work, meditation, or just plain rest. Research more ideas online and you will stumble upon exactly what suits your needs and desires. Blessed Be your new altar.

divine being, the Sun." In other words, color and vibration are the basis of creating everything.

ON YOUR ALTAR: This section will include a variety of items you may want to add to your altar in order to enhance its power. That may include items associated with the ray's corresponding angel, archetype, crystal, and symbolic representations. It is totally up to you to create a special place for your items, symbols, and practice tools. Always keep in mind that this is YOUR sacred space, and you can add as many things as we suggest to your sacred space. You can even change the items out for each day when the ray concentration changes. Figure that the power of the ray color guides your direction and actions.

WORKING WITH YOUR RAY: This collection of exercises and rituals will help you put your knowledge of the ray's power into practice. That could include spells and invocations, chakra work, divination tools such as pendulums and tarot cards, and suggestions for working with plant magic. This includes ways to include your outside environment, like a garden or flower bed, and plant the colors of the rainbow in any design you prefer. Like attracts like, so your flowers will attract the vibrations of the color we see and contain the extra magic of that color of the rainbow. You will be surrounded by these light waves and enhanced by their presence inside and out.

Each chapter will also include a sidebar on a branch of witchcraft—of which there are many—that you may want to incorporate.

INITIATION: This is a special ritual that you should use when you decide to begin establishing meaningful connection to your ray of choice. It will open you up to its power and allow it to begin flowing through you.

MAGICAL BIRDS AND THE RAINBOW WITCH

Birds have been celebrated in legend, story, and witchcraft since time began. They intrigued early humans because they fly. As such, they were believed to magically touch the heavens, be privy to secrets, and possess supernatural powers as they disappeared into the clouds between this world and the realms humans can only dream about. They were believed to carry messages from humanity to the deities above. We have called birds holy and sacred, made gods of them, and worshipped at their altars. And now the Rainbow Witch brings their hidden powers into our magical circle for the purpose of casting spells, dispensing blessings, and conjuring transformations. One bird for each ray.

Seven birds sit on the points of the star, the Phoenix, the Pheasant, the Raven, the Peacock, the Roc, the Falcon, and the Caladrius. As you investigate each of the seven rays, you will read about its corresponding magical birds.

By the time you have finished this book, and the empowering processes in it, you will be well-equipped to establish yourself as a full-fledged Rainbow Witch. The information in these pages is meant to help you begin to understand mystery, magic, and how the inner powers of the universe work. Although no one can truly comprehend the many-faceted splendor of the natural world, by connecting to these seven rays, you can begin to open yourself to their power. This book, and the practices with it, is a salute to witchcraft, nature, and everything alive—past, present, and future.

Welcome to the Rainbow Witch classroom. I hope you will enjoy and benefit from the collection of these sacred studies and practices.

We all share the same rainbow. Surround yourself with its colors and drink in the majesty and power the colors offer you.

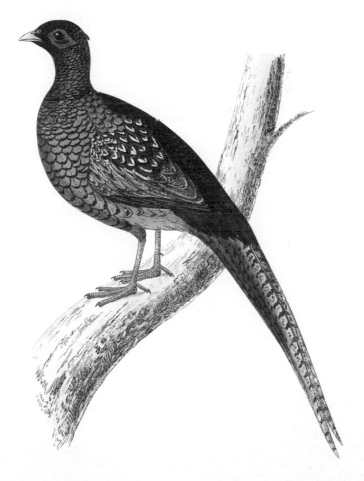

Chapter 1

THE RED RAY

JANUARY 1—FEBRUARY 21.
THE DAY OF THE WEEK IS MONDAY.

WHEN WE THINK OF THE FIRST RAY, RED, WE THINK OF IMAGES THAT can be charged with drama: a bull charging at a red flag, a red light at an intersection, a red firetruck racing to put out a blaze. Bright red in the natural world can indicate alarm, like the hot energy of the lava flowing down a coal black mountainside. And the color red can incite passion, intrigue, and mystery: ruby red lipstick for the dance, Dorothy's red shoes in the *Wizard of Oz*, red lanterns decorating the streets at Chinese New Year. Oh, the color red—it stirs the emotions, doesn't it? There's nothing peaceful and calm about red. It shouts, "Hey, get up and dance!"

Because the red ray is the color of love it can teach us about service to others and universal compassion. Using the light of the red ray will help you find the empathy you seek to develop and use the knowledge you have been given to raise your own vibration and the vibration of others. With this ray you have been given the power, courage, and drive to discover the true meaning of your life. Ask for inspiration using any of the red-related people or symbols to open your receptors and receive the answers you seek. Be patient: the red ray will only enlighten the true seeker. It will give you enlightenment once you have professed your true path. In Alice Bailey's esoteric writings on color, she shares her thoughts about red: "*Red* is for all apparent purposes one of the most difficult colours to consider. It ranks as undesirable. Why? Because it has been considered as the colour of kama, or evil desire, and the picture of the dark and lurid reds in the emotional body of the undeveloped man rises ever to one's vision. Yet—at some distant time—red will be the basis of a solar system, and in the perfect merging of red, green and blue will come eventually the completed work of the Logos." Remember, red is the color of X-rays and it can see right through you. Be authentic with this color and your quest.

ON YOUR ALTAR

When you work magic under the red ray, you may want to use the symbols of it on your altar, incorporate red flowers or the items mentioned below.

RED RAY ANGEL

If your practice includes angels, you might want to know that Archangel Uriel's ray is pure red light. Archangel Uriel stands for truth and wisdom. He is guardian of the direction north, which represents earth, home, security, fertility. He comes to us when we seek wisdom or ask for answers, and he helps us put that wisdom into action toward the service of others. If you are seeking help with any of the above, ask Archangel Uriel to come to you on the days that the red ray is most potent.

HOW TO CALL IN AN ANGEL

Select a time that is still and quiet. Between midnight and 3:00 a.m. is a good time to reach the angels.

Sit near your altar and light a white candle for you and a colored candle according to the rays for the angel you want to reach. It is advised to have an image of the angel on your altar.

Take a few moments to clear your chakras by meditation, chanting, or smudging with sage. When you feel you are balanced, ask the pendulum if the time is right. Yes or No. If you can play some music or use chimes, that will signal the upper realm you wish contact.

When you feel the mood has been set, say:

ANGEL REALM,

PLEASE HEAR MY CALL

I WISH TO SPEAK WITH [NAME YOUR ANGEL]

MOST OF ALL.

WITH A SACRED HEART I DO REACH

FOR THE ANGEL [NAME], WHOM I SEEK.

COME TO ME THIS VERY NIGHT.

I ASK FOR HELP

AND SEEK INSIGHT.

IF YOU WOULD VISIT ME THIS NIGHT

ALL IS WELL AND ALL IS RIGHT.

WELCOME [NAME OF ANGEL].

Wait now. In peace and patience, wait. The angel world is full of requests, and they might be helping someone else. Don't worry. Sit in silence for thirty minutes and wait for them. If they do not appear, it means only this is not the night. Sometimes angels appear as a breeze, as a light tap on the shoulder, maybe even a kiss on the cheek. You must stay sensitive to any slight change in the environment, because that is a sign an angel is nearby. When you feel that shift, a good practice is to form prayer hands and give them a slight bow. Now you may speak with them. State what is on your mind. Please remember their answers may not be literal or in words. Sometimes it is, but you may need to help them along. When angels speak with humans, they have to lower their vibrations. As such, they might need to move things around or "show" you their reply. Again, make it easy for them. They might communicate with you through the pendulum, they might work through you with automatic writing. I like to have all of those things available to make communication easier. Some people give up too easily and aren't willing to tune into the angel's frequency. The higher you lift yourself, the clearer the communication will be. If you have a request for them that doesn't require an answer, that's fine, too. Please remember, that angels and entities answer our summons. They appreciate you raising your vibration to make their journey easier. Be sure to show gratitude, appreciation, and delight. Angels like smiles and happy hearts.

When you have concluded your session—be sure to honor their workload—give them a special tribute.

YOUR TIME TONIGHT HAS FILLED MY SOUL

YOUR GRACE A SIGHT TO BEHOLD

EXCHANGE OF LOVE FOR SHARING GIFTS

OUR TIME IS SHORT AND PARTING SWIFT

I HONOR AND PLEDGE FIDELITY TO YOU

FOR WHO YOU ARE AND ALL YOU DO.

BLESSED BE.

RED RAY ARCHETYPE

If you work with archetypes, red would be the color of the Hero whose main feat in life is to overcome the monster of darkness in the expected triumph of consciousness over the unconscious. Summon your inner Hero when the red ray is most potent.

RED RAY DIVINE ENERGY

You may like working with god and goddess energy in your practice. If so, the ones representing the color red are Ares, Mars, Bridget, Hestia, Vesta, Chantico, Mahuea, Ishat, Huilu, and Sekhmet. These are the movers and shakers of history past, and they made a big impact in their days of glory. Place a picture or statue of them on your altar when you are working with the red ray. You may also choose to connect with animal gods and goddesses, such as Bastet, Ganesh, or Anubis. Dedicate your time and your practice to them as sacred moments. You can also enhance your connection to these deities with lit incense, burning palo santo, or frankincense resin on a charcoal tablet. By invoking their power, you also enhance the work you are doing. Red energy moves things along.

RED RAY ASTROLOGY

Astrologically, Aries is the first sign of the zodiac. Aries is ruled by Mars, the God of War, who is represented by the color red. Aries is ruled by the planet Mars, which is also associated with the attributes of power and conquest. Aries and the color red also mean beginnings and forward motion. If you look up into the sky, the Aries constellation is located in the Northern celestial hemisphere between Pisces to the west and Taurus to the east. The name *Aries* is Latin for "ram." The color red also represents the Sun, Aries, and Mars. Using the red ray during the time of Aries would ensure the greatest cosmic attention to your efforts.

RED RAY CHAKRA

Just as the color red is associated with the first sign of the zodiac, so too is the color associated with the first or root chakra. The root chakra, *Muladhara*, is located at the base of the spine. The word means "root," and is associated with the earth element, which is linked to how firmly you feel rooted in your life. Its associated color is red, hence its links to fire and hearth. The hearth is an ancestral symbol where all the family gathered together to enjoy each other, form familial bonds, share food and support, nourish and care for each other. This chakra includes your family relationships, your sense of security, grounding, and personal power. We hold our beliefs in this chakra and it influences our thinking. When this chakra is balanced, we feel alive, happy, optimistic, grounded, vital, and motivated. When it is unbalanced, we may experience depression, confusion, alienation, jealousy, self-centeredness, aggression, or rage. This balance is important for our bones, adrenal glands, colon, and spinal column—those things that hold us up. To cleanse this chakra and balance it, practice Ujjayi or victorious breath. Use physical exercises for the legs and core to strengthen this chakra. Learn how to breathe to enhance your physical power. Exercise is a key to relaxation of pent-up anger, frustration, and emotion. The more you release the negative, the sooner you will create room for the positive in the form of love to fill that open space.

UJJAYI BREATH

Here are instructions for Ujjayi breathing for root chakra work.

- ✦ Keep your mouth closed.

- ✦ Constrict your throat to the point that your normal breathing makes a rushing noise, that sounds like the ocean.

- ✦ Control your breath with your diaphragm.

- ✦ Keep your inhalations and exhalations equal in duration.

Breathe like this slowly and evenly for approximately thirty seconds. Check for light-headedness. Continue if it feels right.

RED RAY FLOWER ESSENCES

Should you be so inclined, in the Bach Flower tradition, Impatiens is the flower remedy that helps us to be less frustrated and hasty with others. It is part of Dr. Bach's original Crisis Formula that assists with calming agitated thoughts and emotions. It is perfect to assist the root chakra in cleansing and healing.

RED RAY ESSENTIAL OILS

On a gentler level than raging fire, we have essential oils associated with the red ray. The leaders are red mandarin, red thyme, red basil, black pepper, neroli and chili oil. The red energy herbs are rosemary, copal, palm, and sunflower. The plants empowered by the red ray are red poppy, red dianthus, red ginger, red basil, Hawaiian red ginger plant root, and red rose. When you use these oils on your body (diluted) you will attract the red ray, which can mean anything from more love in your life to more energy, healing family issues, and increased power to seek what you desire.

RED RAY CRYSTALS

All crystals and gemstones associated with this first ray fall into the red hues. They would be ruby, red coral, garnet, carnelian, red jasper, red agate, red tourmaline, red apatite, red diamond, and eudialyte, which are the main red stones associated with the red ray and properties. You may find others, too. Having those crystals and stones around you will enhance the presence of the red ray. You can wear them, place them on your altar, or incorporate them as part of your spell work to enhance the presence of red ray energy.

RED RAY SYMBOLS

Archetypes and symbols animate the subconscious and generate a response deep within our inherited psychological DNA. Red ray symbols are powerful and mysterious, associated with dynamism and action. To connect with red ray energy, try focusing on the jaguar, lion, or dragon, the powerful, dramatic animals in the jungle. Other powerful images that can help generate red ray energy are the arrow, the oak tree, and any natural feature with fearsome power such as Niagara Falls. Because these powerful forces are classified as yang in Feng Shui, they have a masculine energy that aligns with the red ray. For those who fancy ancient alphabets, the Celtic Ailm is the twentieth letter of the ancient Celtic alphabet, Ogham, and is associated with longevity, strength, and endurance, and can also be an effective visualization for channeling the red ray.

RED RAY FENG SHUI

In Chinese medicine and Feng Shui, the color red is associated with the element of Fire. Fire typically moves upward and is viewed as dynamic, energetic, passionate, enterprising, and often destructive energies. It also represents heat, summer, and enthusiasm, nature at its peak of growth, and warmth in human relationships. As with every element in Feng Shui practice there is a yang version and a yin version. Wild and uncontained flames are a more yang representation of the color red, while a candle flame would be more yin.

WORKING WITH THE RED RAY

When you work with the red ray, know that you are releasing power and force into the universe. If you are having a down day, not feeling well, or are distracted, this would not be a good day to work with the red ray. Be sure you are energetic and totally prepared to direct this powerful color and energy to where you want it. It's like having a team of enthusiastic horses saddled up and ready to go with no driver in sight. It's a good idea to do some energizing physical movements, get your blood coursing, and then embark on working with the red ray. When you complete your work with the red ray, be sure to hydrate yourself, take a rest, cool down with a walk in the woods, sit in a garden or a park, and allow that red energy to cool off. If you don't have access to a pool that you can jump into and take a few laps, then run through the sprinkler a few times and water down the potency.

These practices can help you channel the powerful energy of the red ray.

RED RAY LOVE SPELL

Cast this powerful love spell during the period between January 1 and February 21.

First, call on the powers of Archangel Uriel and fire goddess Vesta.

Light a red candle, diffuse red thyme essential oil and in your burning vessel, light some dried red basil sprinkled with a pinch of paprika. Keep rose essential oil on hand. When it has burned and gone out, say:

> Earnest love I send you
>
> Along the red, red ray
>
> My perfect love receives it
>
> On this very day.
>
> Guard these fires Vesta,
>
> As Uriel brings them here
>
> And we will know we're meant to be
>
> Forever and a year.

Close by thanking all entities who helped with this spell casting. Gather the ashes and place them in a small cotton bag with a red tourmaline, red ruby, or red jasper gemstone. Tie the bag with a red ribbon or string. Drop three drops of red thyme on the bag and wear it on your person for three days. Your true love will feel the call.

RED RAY DIVINATION

For tarot afficionados, the red ray is represented by The Emperor, The Tower, and Death, all powerful and life-changing energies. Use these cards in your red ray spells. Have them present. For an overview of tarot card meanings, refer to the appendix on page 212.

The divination tool for the red ray is the pendulum.

PENDULUMS ARE LIKE DOLPHINS

When dolphins are trained to jump on command, the trainers begin by placing a bar in the water. They encourage the dolphins to swim over the bar. If they do, they are rewarded with a fish. After the dolphins master this activity, the trainer gradually raises the bar. Each time the dolphins successfully jump over the bar, they get a fish reward. If the dolphins swim under the bar, nothing happens. No fish, no yelling—they just know that they should try again. As the bar is raised higher and higher, the dolphins continue to be rewarded for every successful jump they make over the bar.

We train our subconscious to use the pendulum in the same way. We use praise and reward to our subconscious when it responds and gives us an answer to our question. When the subconscious is praised, it will continue to respond to the question when asked. This does not mean we only praise the subconscious when we get the answer we want to hear, but we do so every time there is a clear response, whether it is negative or positive or what we are hoping for or afraid of. Using a pendulum is a wonderful way to get to the roots of our internal belief systems and dig deeper into who we are, using the red ray to get there.

PENDULUM MAGIC OF THE RED RAY

When we use a pendulum, we are raising the curtains on our intuitive reservoirs and using our natural intuition to speak to us through a device that can give us solutions to the specific questions we ask. Divination with a pendulum allows us to understand life more clearly. It helps us take the guesswork out of inner guidance by serving up clear answers to selected questions. We use the pendulum to unlock natural

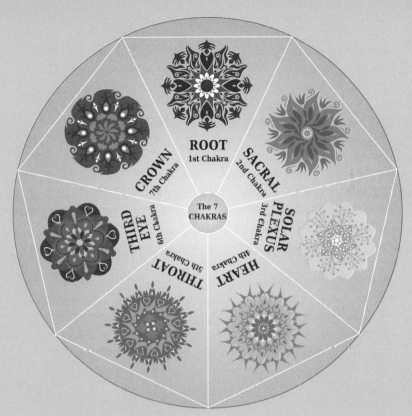

Chart to use with your pendulum.

wisdom that we might otherwise not pay much attention to or may overlook entirely.

Use the chart above to see if your root chakra is overactive or underactive. You can use it as you move through the remaining rays in your book, too.

RED RAY PLANT MAGIC

Consider consecrating part of your garden to the red ray if you want to include your exterior environment in your Rainbow Witchcraft practice. You can empower your spells with red ray energy and use the flowers in your activities. Plant red flowers in early spring. This could be on a special weekday when the frost is gone and planting is encouraged for your region. Grow tomatoes when the ground is past freezing. Plant red thyme, sunflowers, holly, roses, and poppies. If your weather permits, plant on the spring equinox for good results, and dedicate your garden to the red ray of the rainbow. Plant red tulips on the winter solstice or the autumnal equinox, depending on your region.

If you want to plant a tree that embodies the energies of the red ray, choose a dragon's blood tree, *Dracaena cinnabari*, which is also known as the Socotra dragon tree. It is native to the Socotra Archipelago, part of Yemen, located in the Arabian Sea, and it is named after the blood-like color of the red sap that the trees produce. If you choose to grow one, make sure it gets bright sunlight but never direct sun for extended hours. Provide it with a few hours of morning or late evening sunlight. (And never harvest the red sap from the tree trunk, as it is poisonous.)

RED RAY MAGICAL BIRD

Animals of the red ray tend to be powerful and awe-inspiring. The most closely aligned may be the phoenix, a mythical bird from ancient Greek and Egyptian mythology. It was said that this bird lived for five hundred years, and right before its time was about to end, it constructed a beautiful nest in which it immolated itself. From these ashes, a new phoenix arose to live another five hundred years. In this dramatic way, the phoenix holds and embodies the energy of the red ray, which is associated with both destruction and creation.

The phoenix gives us the power to clearly define our lives and magical practices and shows us that transformation is possible and there is life ever after, ongoing, and self-determined. There are many legends about the phoenix, but its power to reinvent itself and come back stronger has been the inspiration for poets, musicians, philosophers, and leaders for centuries. Where in your life can you use phoenix ingenuity and bravery? The phoenix will provide the inspiration and support for whatever changes you want to make.

PHOENIX MAGIC

Find a yellow feather. Paint the outside tips red. On the upper part, draw a magic third eye using blue, green, or black paint. Make as many of these feathers as you want.

Draw a circle for your magic. Set up your altar, if you use one, and be sure to include an image of a phoenix. Place the feather in your dominant hand. Take your wand in the other hand. Lightly tap the feather three times to summon this amazing mythical creature. Speak the following incantation aloud, tapping after each line.

> Join me, mighty phoenix spirit.
>
> Bring your golden aura here and enter my circle.
>
> Ignite my powers of determination and transformation.
>
> (Clearly state your intention here of what you want transformed.)

Put the wand down. Then, using the feather, form three circles in the air. Speak these words aloud with each circle:

CIRCLE ONE: *With your feather I summon the past, I thank it and release it, and banish it forever.*

CIRCLE TWO: *I acknowledge the present as we stand in your powerful presence, mighty phoenix.*

CIRCLE THREE: *I now summon the future, enthusiastically inviting transformation to manifest in full color and blinding glory, that we may live and experience what we have proclaimed. Manifest now.*

In honor of the powerful phoenix, may this renovation and new life become the reincarnation of all that we have claimed. Pick up your wand.

In gratitude for your powers and assistance, I bow to you, O mighty phoenix and thank you for your generous and most kind assistance. I claim it thus here and now it becomes. Blessed Be. Tap the feather and place it in its holder.

If you wish to say more to the phoenix, please do so. The above is only a guideline for your summoning ceremony.

RED RAY WITCHCRAFT

You may wish to explore other witch practices that fall under the dynamics and attributes of the red ray. Here are just a few that may appeal to you: A Chaos Witch places complete faith in themselves alone and have no attachments to rituals, deities, dogma, or binding objects or practices of faith. Dianic Witches are modern Pagans who use the tradition of the Goddesses for empowerment. They follow Diana the Warrior Goddess. Of course, the Fire Witch has to fall into this category because they work directly with the elements of fire, coals, and wood, and believe in purification by flame. The Gardnerian Witch follows order, structure, and high organization according to the founder Gerald Gardner. The Hereditary Witch also falls under this ray because they were born into witchcraft and use the handed-down teachings from family witches. The Tech Witch is also red ray because they use digital devices, which are considered the fire element in Chinese lore, in their practice of magic. Lastly, the Traditional Witch is red ray because they come from the British Isles and are based in older traditions and not influenced by modern witch practices. They are, in that way, the root chakra of witch work.

INITIATION INTO THE RED RAY

Because the root chakra is so closely tied to red ray energy, this initiation will focus on deepening that connection.

As we mentioned before, the first chakra holds the old beliefs, and ideas you were taught in childhood, all of which are deeply embedded into the tissue structure and emotional memories from the past. Accessing the root chakra brings up family issues, invisible ties to the past, and relationships we've had that govern how we feel about ourselves. The work begins here to uncover what no longer serves us and to replace the old thoughts, beliefs, and opinions with the way we choose to think and feel today.

To begin your initiation into red ray energy, you will first need to clear your root chakra. For the clearing process, you will want to gather a red metal bucket, a red journal, a red pen, your favorite passionate music, a red candle, a red crystal, a red herb, an icon or picture of Archangel Uriel, a god or goddess from the red family, and a red flower. You may choose to sit on a red mat or one with the rainbow colors. You can even put on a red shirt, a red scarf, red socks, or red undies.

First, take time to work with the root chakra. This should take about twenty minutes, minimum, although you can stay here for as long as you need. You can approach your root chakra work in a number of ways: it could be as simple as sitting still, allowing the intensity of the moment to gather and allowing it to be fully present within you. You could choose to open with some Ujjayi breathing to release any and all tension. Yoga can also be helpful, as it is a wonderful way to elongate the muscles and stretch out the muscle fibers holding the memories of the past. Qigong and Tai Chi have similar effects, because they harmonize and balance the muscles and the emotions of the body during practice.

Spiritually and emotionally, inner-child work can be another long-term way to clear your root chakra, as it emphasizes tackling beliefs from the past that may be deeply buried. You can find a therapist who specializes in this type of work to dig in deep.

Meditation is another wonderful way to heal any wounds carried in the root chakra. Choose the method you like best and carve out at least twenty minutes. Allow your thoughts to surface and, without judging them, let them disappear into the ether. Usually, once the mind serves up problems, it then settles into peace and plainness. This is your chance to fill it with what you really want to be thinking about. This state is where healing takes place, and where you can become the driver rather than the passenger of your mind.

One good way to combine root chakra or red ray practices is to burn some palo santo, diffuse some red thyme oil, bring out a red tourmaline crystal, light a red candle, find a statue of a lion, hold a yoga practice or a qigong session, and then write about your impressions with a red pen in your red journal. Sit under your dragon's blood tree and put on some music that stirs the passions in your soul (mine is Celtic Thunder), and allow yourself to be symbolically swallowed up by the color red. Stay there as long as you can for as long as it takes. Don't move forward until you have mastered the red ray.

A Rainbow Witch values this process and does whatever it takes to balance the crucial root chakra. This is the beginning and the base upon which we will build the rest of the rays. Invest the time to explore your root chakra and get to know what it is holding within.

When you are satisfied with the root chakra work you have done, pick up a red metal bucket and add slips of paper that represent what you no longer want to believe or feel. Then, safely, light a match and drop it into the bucket. Watch as the flames burn the papers to ash. After the fire is safely extinguished, write about your experience in your red journal. Take thirty minutes or more to capture your experience in your red notebook using your red pen. What did you feel as you were writing down what you wished to banish? How did it affect you to see these thoughts, feelings, and situations disappear into the fire? Describe how you feel about the red ray and the root chakra. Detail your feelings and what you may have learned. Be sure to snag these feelings and impressions right away when they are fresh. Waiting will only dilute your memory and the significance of these exercises. Make any notes you wish so you can revisit if you feel you are out of balance in any way with the root chakra. It is critical to keep this chakra in balance all the time, so you are in control of your life and future in a powerful way.

The cleansing you experience will immerse you in the light of the red ray, the first color of the rainbow.

Chapter 2

THE ORANGE RAY

FEBRUARY 22–APRIL 14.
THE DAY OF THE WEEK IS TUESDAY.

TAKE THE HOT PASSION OF THE RED RAY AND MIX IT WITH THE JOY and mellow wisdom of the activating yellow ray, and what do you get in between? The orange ray. Orange is generally a happy-making color. Just as we love the smell of orange blossoms in the spring and the sweet and healthy juice of this perfectly sun-ripened fruit, orange is an inviting and joyous color. It suggests warmth, heat, sunshine, enthusiasm, creativity, success, encouragement, transition, transformation, determination, good health, and active stimulation. It is a bright and happy color that denotes fun and happiness, sexuality, freedom, youth, expression, creativity, and fascination. It is the signature color of the extrovert. Everyone needs a little dose of orange each day—for the fun, if not for the vitamin C.

ON YOUR ALTAR

When you assemble your orange ray altar, consider incorporating representations of some of the following corresponding energies.

ORANGE RAY ANGEL

The Archangel Chamuel is the angel most associated with the orange ray. Noted for banishing Adam and Eve from the garden because greed got in their way, he is a symbol of being true to yourself. Chamuel wants you to have confidence in your own abilities, banish the ties that bind you, and replace them with enthusiasm so you can cherish the bonds of friendships and experience true intimacy. He heightens your faith and brings love, adventure, and creativity with him. He is the personal messenger of inspiration and desire, and monitors excesses of craving and avarice. Chamuel can help you sort out any questions about truth, morality, ethics, standards, principles, and the choices you might want to make to stay on the right side of them. He's your supportive guide through all of the temptations the world may put in your path.

ORANGE RAY ASTROLOGY & COSMOLOGY

The planet Mercury brings heightened thinking capacity to daily activities, oversees the fine arts and sciences, and helps us make clear decisions even in confusing times. Mercury is also the planet that connects mind, body, and soul, which is both creative and practical at the same time. If

BLACK AND WHITE

Black and white can be included as candle on your altar, if you like. These two hues are not considered to be colors, however, and do not constitute rays of the rainbow, because black is the absence of light, and white contains all the wavelengths of visible light.

you're looking for orange in the night sky, Aldebaran is the brightest star in the constellation and is known as the "Eye of Taurus." Slightly brighter Betelgeuse, the shoulder of Orion, is a little farther to the left of the moon. If you look closely, you'll notice that both stars are orange, two rare specks of color in the night sky. When these appear in the night sky, you will know the orange ray is activated.

ORANGE RAY ARCHETYPE

The Revolutionary embodies the courage, passion, and joy of the impulse to change the world. Revolutionaries are keys to improvement and shifting the status quo. New ideas take flight and consciousness is raised with this archetype. This will help you if you are thinking about social change, or change in the family, relationships, business, or anything that might need a dose of fresh air and new thinking.

ORANGE RAY CHAKRA

Orange is the color of the second chakra, *Swadisthana*, the naval chakra, which guides our capacity to understand. This is the place where we go to clear our thoughts and to make sure we are congruous in body, mind, and soul. Think of this chakra as a bridge bringing all our parts together and creating the outward expression of our deepest mortal desires. The second chakra is the center of our moral code. We are taught beliefs in the first chakra, and in the second we process them and make them our own. For any belief that doesn't serve you, replace it with a better one that does.

ORANGE RAY FLOWER ESSENCES

If you enjoy the vibrational qualities of Bach Flowers, the remedies for this chakra correspond to the emotions of fear and self-awareness: cherry plum, gentian, and mimulus. Cherry plum relieves fears and inner tension, as well as the inability to make decisions. Gentian can be used to alleviate feelings of unworthiness or discouragement. Mimulus inspires courage. These remedies can help strengthen your second chakra and the collection of those thoughts and beliefs that make you unique and special.

ORANGE RAY CRYSTALS

The most effective stones for aligning with the color orange are orange themselves: amber, andesine, fire opal, sunstone, Mexican fire opal, sapphire padparadscha, orange diamond, orange calcite, orange aventurine, carnelian, and agate are just some of the many orange crystals that make great additions to an orange ray altar. Individually, these stones have a variety of uses, but due to their color, they also resonate with joy and bravery, and help to strengthen one's resolve and thinking patterns. They can bring you a balance of motivation and assurance. Orange calcite, for example, is a complex blend of both.

ORANGE RAY SYMBOLS

If the color orange was interpreted as a symbol, it would include fertility symbols like the Ankh, the Celtic Dragon, the Horned God, the Lingam, and Yoni. Add to that list the apple eaten by Adam and Eve, given its association to Archangel Chamuel, who banished them from Eden for indulging in it. And of course you can't go wrong with adding an orange to your altar, because it represents health and nature and is bursting with

During the celebration of Chinese New Year, it is common to make offerings of oranges. Since this period is a time for new beginnings, oranges are a customary way to call in good fortune and wealth. Small orange trees or kumquat trees are often placed in doorways to welcome fortune inside. In remembrance of an emperor who gave gifts of oranges to his people at the New Year, oranges are freely given to friends and business associates.

goodness. Similarly, anything representing a phallus can be useful in promoting orange's generative energy. The mythical mermaid is a joyful symbol of orange's capacity for transition and change.

ORANGE RAY ESSENTIAL OILS

The essential oils related to the color orange include, unsurprisingly, sweet orange, bitter orange, tangerine, and kumquat. Neroli, calendula, marigold, and tagetes essential oils are also orange in hue, so can be good additions to your altar. Keep in mind that tagetes must be used sparingly as it is toxic to many, especially pregnant women. Orangish carrot seed oil is also one to consider, on its own or as an addition to many cosmetic and grooming products. Orange oils bring a brightness and a soothing energy at the same time. There is nothing like sweet orange to brighten your day and open your mind.

ORANGE RAY PLANT MAGIC

A garden filled with bright orange nasturtiums is a springtime sight to behold. Sitting under the boughs of an African tulip can be a magnificent second chakra indulgence. They can be grown in any non-freezing part of the world. Other orange floral gorgeousnesses are begonias, bird of paradise, buddleia, calendula, marigold, California poppy, canna lily, chrysanthemum, daylily, ranunculus, cosmos, dahlia, lantana, helenium, pansies, and many, many more. Planting any of those, based on your location, adds vibrancy and joy to your garden, especially for the faeries, who adore nasturtiums because they can sleep under their wide, green, umbrella-like leaves. Surround yourself with orange blooms and sense how your mood automatically rises.

ORANGE RAY DIVINE ENERGY

Gaia is the most prominent goddess associated with oranges because she represents earth and creation, where the fruits grow. Arausio was a local Celtic water god who gave his name to the town of Arausio (now the modern city of Orange) in southern Gaul. Enlil, the god of earth, was associated with oranges because of their globe-like shape. Hephaestus, the volcano god, is a strong deity to channel while aligning with this ray because orange is the color of molten lava.

Rather than adding images of these specific gods to your altar, or perhaps in addition to them, you might consider adding an orange peel. Orange peel has long been associated with abundance and the attraction of money in addition to an offering to the gods. It is also a popular choice for spell work in many practices of witchcraft.

ORANGE RAY HERBS

Orange herbs include orange mint, sea buckthorn, carrot tops, and marigolds. Carrot tops, which have a peppery flavor, are similar to arugula or parsley and can bring that same sort of spice to a range of dishes. When cooking with them, remove the fibrous stems, as you would with any other tender herb such as parsley or dill. Some enjoy topping their salads with nasturtium blossoms because they have a peppery taste that adds a zing to the other ingredients.

ORANGE RAY FENG SHUI

The Feng Shui representation of orange is a blend of fire and earth elements, which means it is passionate, joyful, and grounded at the same time: a combination of the qualities of red and yellow that make its hue. If you think of it emotionally, you can say orange is solid like earth, yet has the motivation and force of red—the best of both colors.

WORKING WITH THE ORANGE RAY

Here are some practices that you can use to work with orange ray energy. The orange ray carries with it stabilizing gravity and forward movement at the same time. It contains the power for change and motivation, as well as the energy of earth, which means it will keep your wildest desires on the right track. Be sure to do some grounding exercises or meditation before working with this ray. They can be as simple as taking a walk or doing jumping jacks. The point is to honor the fire in this color while maintaining a connection to solid earth. Orange ray energy isn't impulsive: it is powerful and steady. Use it when you have a plan, and you need support to move that plan forward. It wants you to organize your thoughts and only step into action when you have all your ducks in a row. Orange requires patience, planning, and steady execution, so use this energy to make your dreams come true one step at a time.

ORANGE RAY DIVINATION

The tarot cards representing the orange ray are The Sun, The Hierophant, and The Lovers.

SACRAL CHAKRA WORK

Getting in touch and working with your second chakra is one of the keys to mastering the orange ray. The sacral chakra is extremely important because it is believed to govern the human experience of personal sexuality, methods of creative expression, interior emotions, and the capacity to experience the joy and magnificence of life. The second chakra is home to self-esteem and happiness. According to most traditions, it can become blocked and unbalanced, as can the other chakras in the body. According to Alice Bailey, the force of orange comes in to perfect the link between spirit and form, between life and the vehicles through which it is seeking expression.

On the physical level, the second chakra controls the kidneys, the ovaries, the testes, and the uterus. As a result, when the second chakra is blocked or unbalanced, one can experience lower back pain, urinary complications, stiffness, kidney pain, infertility, or impotency. The emotions of pleasure, sense of well-being, enjoyment of life, sexual expression, and capacity for abundance are stymied. If your second chakra is overactive you can have symptoms of creating excess drama, you may be highly emotional or clingy, or you may find yourself moody and overstep personal boundaries. An underactive second chakra leads to a sense of worthlessness, being closed off to others, stiff, unemotional, and lacking the self-esteem to succeed in life. That's why this is a fairly significant chakra to get back in balance if it is askew.

For this chakra, self-help books and audio are excellent. Anything that raises your self-esteem, confidence and *I deserve it all* attitude. Fill the room with the aroma of orange essential oil (tangerine or neroli work well) and give yourself a loving sound bath. Spend this time concentrating and deeply listening to the music or lyrics of positive songs. Take them into your heart. Picture yourself as that singer, having the ability to say those things about yourself. Here are some suggestions, but there are more if you search for songs about self-love and self-esteem. "Video" by India Arie, "Unpretty" by TLC, "Born This Way" by Lady Gaga, "Roar" by Katy Perry, "Rise Up" by Andra Day, "Who You Are" by Jessie J, "Scars to Your Beautiful" by Alessia Cara, "Crooked Smile" by J. Cole. Spotify has several categories where you can find self-esteem and self-confidence recordings.

ORANGE RAY SYMBOLS

Carl Jung and Joseph Campbell are famous for assessing that our human unconscious resides on a mythical level, and it is frequently triggered by symbols that have universal meaning beyond the confines of language. We respond to symbols both current and ancient with an unspoken, inner wisdom that predates even our birth in this lifetime. When symbols are used in witchcraft, spells, and rituals, they bring with them an ancient power that intensifies what one witch can do, by adding the power of ancestors when they used the same symbols in their magic long ago.

Practicing witches are connected to each other by using certain symbols in their work that represent universal energies and have proven to be commonly accepted worldwide. For example, we have the Greek version of the four elements of the universe as they envisioned life.

These symbols are working today around the world. Even though you may want to change or alter the symbols, consider how powerful it is to connect with the magic of witches all over the world. Try to retain the symbolic mainstays for the sake of energetic unity.

ORANGE RAY PHEASANT MAGIC

To tap into orange ray animal energy, look for the pheasant. The pheasant is a bird that brings protection against evil spirits. Rooted in self-survival because of superior awareness and instincts, pheasants can sense even a hint of danger and make you aware of it. But they are also confident and joyful: pheasants are proud of their plumage and flaunt it flamboyantly to attract a mate. They are the most self-confident of all birds and balance beauty and exuberance with caution, accumulated knowledge, and awareness. They perfectly embody the orange ray qualities.

Since they cannot fly very high or far, pheasants stay close to the earth. They are swift and cagey so they can outwit and outrun a coyote. They stay close to their homeland: pheasants are social birds and do not migrate. They keep the same mate for life and establish close family ties. Their patience and persistence designate them as orange ray energy through and through. If you happen to see a flock of pheasants together, it is not only a wondrous sight, but it bodes well for you and promises wonderful blessings ahead.

PHEASANT UNIFICATION RITUAL

You will need:

+ One pheasant feather to represent each person you want to unite

+ 10 × 10" piece of orange cloth

+ Orange ribbon to tie the cloth

+ Piece of orange calcite

+ Sprigs of rosemary and parsley

DIRECTIONS

This is a very short yet extremely effective practice to restore bonds with those who have fallen apart or are estranged. Gather your items and place them on the altar. Open your ceremony. Spread the cloth out flat and add one feather for each person. *I bring [name] into this gathering. I bid them welcome, and I promise only peace and friendship will come to them.* Place the feather in the middle of the orange cloth. Add some rosemary and parsley and say, *Loyalty we give to you, love, and fidelity, too. Join with us to feast in joy and evermore our bonds employ.* Repeat these words with each person you want to unite into one community or bring them back into the fold.

When all feathers and herbs have been gathered together, add the piece of orange calcite, tie up the bag, and tap it three times with your pheasant feather. Say, *Now a flock we're sure to be, All hail the pheasant, may Blessed Be.*

Keep the orange bag with feathers and herb suspended in a room where people gather. Tap it three times, three times a day, to reinforce the spell.

ORANGE RAY WITCHCRAFT

Other types of witches falling under the orange ray are: The Alexandrian Witch, who practices rituals following the Qabalah and Enochian magic from United Kingdom. The Chthonioi Witch, who practices according to the Alexandrian tradition of Greek gods and goddesses. The Hellenic Witch, who uses the Greek Pantheon of deities. The Left-Handed Witch, who breaks away from the mold and sets new moral standards. The Norse Witch, who is a seidhr, and uses traditional Nordic deities, like Odin and Freya, to predict the future. The Sun Witch, who uses solar energies, and legends for the basis of their practice. And finally, the Urban Witch, who adapts their practice to the diverse spiritual ecosystem of their natural environment and megapolis.

INITIATION INTO THE ORANGE RAY

Find a container: a metal bucket is good, particularly if it's orange in color. Locate an orange journal, an orange pen, and an orange candle. Consider bringing other items that you may have arranged on your orange ray altar: an orange gemstone or crystal, a representation of the Archangel Chamuel, a symbol like an Ankh. A Celtic dragon image, like a drawing or a figurine, can be immensely helpful here, because the kind of confidence the orange ray can inspire has the force of the mythological dragon.

If you can, wear orange clothing and accessories. And finally, make sure to bring an actual orange, tangerine, or other similarly colored fruit of your choice.

Sit on your mat (which will work best if it is either orange or rainbow in color).

The orange ray is closely aligned with sound—the joyful music that helped you open up your sacral chakra will work here as you clear your mind in preparation for accessing orange ray energy. Use music that makes you rise up inside to open yourself. Any wordless sound that inspires you will do: gongs, Gregorian chant, or instrumentals of any kind are great for this. When you are centered in the feeling of self-importance these sounds provoke, please say these words—the Self-Love Chantra—to yourself five times, slowly:

I am not my feelings.

I am not the opinion of others.

I am divinely appointed. I am chosen. I am star stuff.

I am a perfect expression of the mind, heart, and soul of creation.

I am the real deal.

No person, no thing, and no place can ever hurt me, betray me, or diminish me, and no person, place or thing ever has.

I am totally free of any past thoughts that bind me to a belief of lack or insufficiency.

I am the cream of the crop. I am the top of the heap,

I am all that there is, and all that ever was, and all that there needs to be.

Whole, complete, and perfect. That's me.

What's not to love about that?

Read these words slowly to yourself, repeating louder and louder each time, five times. Eat your orange or tangerine and close this session. Finally, speak the following words:

> May the energies of the orange ray encompass my being, penetrate my soul, and forever hold the balance I need to be aligned so that I can do my best work as a Rainbow Witch. Blessed Be.

When you are done, please take thirty minutes to write about this experience in your orange journal with your orange pen. Include anything you learned or experienced in this activity and write about what the color orange means to you. How did you feel as you were speaking these words? What did the music stir in you? Take your time. Add anything you want about the orange ray and how you feel about it.

Capture in words what your next steps will be and make a note of where you are in your process. Are you content to remain in the orange ray for now, or do you wish to learn more and initiate yourself into an additional ray? Because orange is a color of transition, this is an excellent moment to reevaluate your studies and ask yourself how the knowledge you have acquired may affect your powers moving ahead.

Orange is also a great color for achieving alignment. So if you feel you have been out of balance for a long time, you may want to repeat this exercise until you feel in your blood that you believe in yourself. When you feel centered and confident, you will have the strength of a dragon.

Chapter 3

THE YELLOW RAY

APRIL 15 TO JUNE 5.
THE DAY OF THE WEEK IS WEDNESDAY.

CLOSE YOUR EYES AND PICTURE THE COLOR YELLOW. WHAT POPS into your mind first? Lemons? The Sun? A school bus? Bees? Egg yolks? Number Two pencils? Usually we think of happy, positive things when we think of yellow, but oddly enough yellow can also connote cowardice and condemnation. In some Christian paintings, the color yellow was assigned to Judas Iscariot, the man who betrayed their leader, Jesus. From that tradition came the insult "yellow belly," an old schoolyard taunt for classmates perceived to be chicken. Oh wait! A baby chicken is yellow, too.

The American advertising executive and marketing teacher Frank Baker speaks of yellow as a color of warmth, which stimulates mental and muscle activity. He goes on to say that yellow is associated with success and food—a happy, cheerful, encouraging color. Bright yellow gets your attention, and that's why, before Uber and Lyft, taxicabs were painted yellow. However, researchers claim that a baby will cry more often if their nursery is painted yellow. Clearly yellow unlocks something in us: a strong emotional response equally likely to register as elation as it is fear. According to author and spiritual teacher Louise Hay, the emotion fear is located in the liver, hence the disease of the liver called jaundice, which turns the skin yellow.

The color yellow definitely affects the emotions and the spiritual nature of humans: it calls attention to itself. The qualities of the yellow ray bring wisdom from overlooked, ordinary things and push us to accomplish goals, but mostly so we can gain enlightenment from the wisdom we already have within us. This ray encourages us to find the answers inside ourselves because the light is right there, waiting for us to ask questions and, better yet, discover the answer for ourselves.

The yellow ray provides the self-confidence and the intelligence to explore regions outside us. Yellow energy helps us master what we need to learn and shows us how to apply it to our purposes. Remember, yellow is the sun, the leader, the giver of light— so we can use that light to fully become who we were born to be. Alice Bailey believes yellow is the color of the Buddha, because it harmonizes and marks completion and fruition. Yellow can help you become the most evolved, alert version of yourself, no matter what kind of inspirational or intellectual journey you pursue. Yellow is particularly good for creative people: it coaxes the artist out of us, gives us the courage to explore our talents, and pushes us to create something with them. Think of Vincent van Gogh. Yellow is the energy that drew him into the fields, put a brush in his hand, and said, "Vincent, paint what you feel." Use yellow to enhance your inner wisdom, to ignite confidence within yourself to utilize your intelligence to explore your world and open to the possibilities that lie before you.

ON YOUR ALTAR

Use items or other representations of the color to add the excitement and initiative of the yellow ray to your altar. Bring happiness and wisdom to your sacred space in honor of your personal quest to find the joy in everything you do. Use crystals, flowers, and icons of whatever represents the yellow ray to you.

YELLOW RAY ANGEL

The Archangel Jophiel is most closely aligned with the color yellow. Jophiel embodies wisdom, which lifts us up from our baser, more reactive emotions and into the higher realms. The archangel of conscious thought, she invites us to understand that we can call upon the power and intensity of the bright light of reason within us that is full of radiance—our own personal sun. She teaches us that our conscious minds are a source of living, vital illumination, no matter where our intellect journeys. Jophiel can help you pass a math test, and she can also inspire you to write a symphony or paint a masterpiece. It is certain she was with Van Gogh when he painted his sunflowers. This archangel brings loveliness to the planet and into our lives. She heightens the gift of beauty inside all beings and inspires those who would dabble in motivating works, thought, or artistic expression, particularly those who wish to share those expressions with the world to enjoy. She opens our eyes to see the beauty in everything around us. Seek her guidance to remind you that you already have the answer to whatever it is you seek and to go within to find it. She joins you there to show you how.

YELLOW RAY ARCHETYPE

The archetype for yellow is the Creator. This represents personal inspiration, the stimulation of the mind and senses, and activation of energy from mind, body, and soul. The Creator is brimming with self-confidence and does their work (or play) with cheerfulness and overflowing joy. The Creator gets things rolling and adds a spark to the environment or situation. The Creator represents the beginning of time, when one single thought created the entire universe. Without the Creator there can be nothing else.

YELLOW RAY ASTROLOGY

The astrology for yellow is ruled by the planet Jupiter, the planet of beneficence, abundance, and mental acuity. It is the governor of success, wealth, expansion, and generosity. Jupiter generates excitement, good fortune, and expansive thinking. Jupiter can heal your issues surrounding prosperity and self-confidence. It can increase your creative abilities and energize your efforts.

YELLOW RAY FLOWER ESSENCE

If you wish to tap into delight and elation as you work with the yellow ray, consider adding flower essences to your altar that align with those qualities. In the Bach Flower tradition, agrimony is associated with joy, aspen with security, cerato with making decisions, and mustard with uplifting spirits and building self-confidence. Bach Flowers are not an instant cure, like an aspirin is, but we work with them vibrationally to convert any negative tendencies into positive ones. Use these essences to help you shift your moods, and gradually your go-to emotion will be joy.

YELLOW RAY CRYSTAL

Crystals in the yellow hue are gorgeous and fun. Citrine is a wonderful stone that absorbs negativity and does not need cleansing. Yellow jasper and yellow jade are substantive, topaz is lovely, and I personally favor the yellow diamond. Sulphur is yellow, so that's why crystals growing close to a sulfur deposit take on the yellow color. Yellow apatite, heliodor, and various yellow versions of other stones like tourmaline, calcite, topaz, calcite, chalcedony, agate, lemon quartz, and bumble bee jasper are winners. I can attest to yellow jade as bringing creative inspiration, because I wear my yellow jade bracelet when I write.

YELLOW RAY SYMBOLS

If yellow were a symbol, it would be one associated with brightness, beauty, and positivity: a sun icon, a pyramid shape, a dragonfly, a happy face, a sunflower, two goldfish (for yin-yang harmony). In China a calligraphic symbol called *Shuangxi*, which translates to "double happy," is used as a good luck charm. Consider adding a Shuangxi to your altar, in addition to representations of these other symbols.

YELLOW RAY DIVINE ENERGY

The gods and goddesses attributed to yellow are Demeter, Hermes, Hestia, Gaia, Harmonia, Helios, Ra, Aten, Amun, Atum, Sekhmet, Bast, Lugh, Freyr, and Mithra. Every culture has sun gods and goddesses, so the research will be extensive if you want to locate all of them. All of these entities were worshipped for their power, intelligence, and the favors they granted. They are gentler than the red ray gods and goddesses, but not one ounce less powerful, just different in how they portray themselves to their subjects.

YELLOW RAY ESSENTIAL OILS

The essential oils connected to the yellow ray are helichrysum, rose, yellow mandarin, lemon, citrus, yarrow, lemongrass, citronella, Melissa, and yellow marigold, with a disclaimer for caution with use and no use with pregnancy. These oils are filled with joy and brightness. Melissa, for example, comes from the bees and her aroma is designed to lift you in meditation and transport you into another world. The other yellow ray oils have a more earthy grounding, natural scent. Try them with your spell work and feel the elevation.

It is worth noting, none of these rays or colors should be done in a single day. They are complex exercises woven into the deepest parts of your psyche. It is suggested that you take your time, grow with each ray, and don't just tick them off your list. Really work through them. Take your time, a few days if you need to. If you work these exercises and practices multiple times, you'll find a better balance with each color and a fresh meaning to the vibration and magic of the color. The exercises are meant to immerse you deeply into the hues so you can glean the richness they bring. They are meant to deepen your soul and enhance your magic. To become a Rainbow Witch, you need all the colors and the experience they bring to body, mind, and soul. There is no rush.

YELLOW RAY
FENG SHUI

In Feng Shui, the color yellow is associated with earth. Earth is represented by handmade pottery, the ground, and things that are made from the earth, clay, sand, and stone. It brings generosity, nobility, and helpfulness, in addition to well-being and good luck. The yellow ray is lighter than the orange ray. It assumes you are already grounded in red and orange, so it is lighter. It brings real joy, enlightened purpose, wisdom that is accessible within, and a positive sense of entitlement that we all share in the bounty of the earth and the heavens. Yellow is the fresh ray of sun on the morning grass, the steam lifting from the sea, and the light breaking through the bedroom curtains. Yellow is a giant wake-up color that we all need to get our day started and set the tone that this is a grand, beautiful opportunity for a fresh start. "Hello world, it's yellow here!"

WORKING WITH THE YELLOW RAY

Use the following practices to work with the power of the yellow ray. We can use this color for the light and joy it brings. Also use its intelligence for "bright ideas" and fresh beginnings. Red empowers you; orange guides you, and yellow gives you the optimism to go for it. Bring forth your inner joy and sparkle when you work with the yellow ray.

YELLOW RAY CHAKRA

The yellow ray governs the third chakra, *Manipura*, which means "luscious gem"—a fitting name. Physically, it is located near the center of your body, just above the navel. Spiritually, it represents that part of you that is wise and all-knowing, makes plans, and musters the courage to put them into practice. This is the center for manifestation and therefore of magic. Ideas become real through this chakra. It is where your material purpose is fulfilled. It requires stimulus, positive thinking, and praise to perform at its highest capacity. All honor, courage, compassion, responsibility, and self-esteem live in this chakra.

Manipura regulates the central nervous system, endocrine glands, the liver, pancreas, and metabolic system; all the stuff that makes our bodies work. If it is unbalanced, we can suffer from ulcers, gas, nausea, digestive problems, eating disorders, asthma, nerve pain, infections in the liver or kidneys, and fibromyalgia. Emotional issues that surface when we work with this chakra are self-worth, self-confidence, and the big one, self-esteem.

If this chakra is overactive, you could suffer from being domineering, a know-it-all, aggressive, easy to anger, a perfectionist, and hypercritical of self and others. If it is underactive, you might be passive, indecisive, timid, and lack self-control. Balancing this chakra leads to having a happier life filled with more joy.

YELLOW RAY DIVINATION

The tarot cards compatible with the yellow ray are The Sun, The Fool, The Magician, of course, and Strength.

YELLOW RAY MAGICAL BIRD

To access the magic of the yellow ray, look to the raven. Ravens carry with them the yellow ray qualities of intelligence, loyalty, and clarity. From Norse mythology, we learn of two ravens that served the god Odin. Huginn (H'oo'ginn) meant *thought* and Muninn (M'oo'ninn) represented *mind*. Their job was to fly all over the world and bring back messages to Odin. So what thoughts were being created in minds that Odin needed to know about? What were people manifesting and making happen? Was it war? Prosperity? Love? Peace? Joy? People all over the world were making things happen all the time through their thoughts. Odin wanted in on that. He didn't want to be surprised by those who would steal his kingdom, so he sent his ravens out to bring back the secrets they overheard.

Every morning at sunrise, the birds flew off and then returned at sunset, feeding Odin the information he wanted. As a result of this knowledge, he became a better ruler, wise in his decisions. Odin was referred to as the Raven God in many circles because he supplied protection and positivity and was a clear leader, just like his messenger birds. As a reward for their service, he gave his ravens the gift of speech.

The raven allows us to understand the power of our thoughts, that our thoughts become things, and these manifestations are products of the goings-on in our mind. If we are thinking peaceful, kind thoughts, we give off and attract peace and kindness in our lives. If we do the opposite, we bring in negativity and chaos.

The ravens remind us to think only the thoughts we want to manifest in our lives and to clear our minds so only the thoughts that design the life we want to experience are there.

You can call in one or two ravens for your work and ceremony. I enjoy using both Huginn and Muninn as my guides and instructors because they bring clarity and remind me to think about what I want to manifest and clear out the rest of the mind clutter. You can rely on raven magic to keep your mind focused clearly on what you want to manifest and no other noise.

RAVEN MAGIC

For this ceremony, you will need a raven feather and a raven icon, statue, figurine, or drawing.

Hold your raven feather in your non-dominant hand and use it for any expression, prayer, or incantation you wish.

Join me my raven(s). Come to my altar. Let us make our dreams come to life.

From the thoughts in my mind, I create that which I call reality.

My thoughts become my life.

For this ceremony I welcome raven energy, spirit, insight, and magic.

I believe you have it all and bring is graciously to me.

On this day I put my thoughts directly into action and the One Great Spirit delivers the results, easily, effortlessly, and according to my image and description.

Into this powerful moment, place your claim for yourself or the person you are working with. State your claim as if it has already happened. See it and feel it, then say it:

[Clearly state your claim.]

Once you have stated it, read this letter aloud from the One Great Spirit to you:

My dearest, I am fulfilling your imagined results, and stated desires. That is my job to follow your direction. Your job is to align your actions by what you have stated and live as though it had already occurred. Get busy. Do your part in making this happen. I work with the unseen forces, and you work in the world going forth and moving in the right direction as you have described. This is magic in action. I will follow your lead from my place in the cosmos if you go out into your world knowing your dreams are being answered. We are partners in each and every moment, creating and making aspirations real. I'm already at work on your behalf. Be blessed.

Use your feather to stir the air above your head.

With the magic of the raven(s) and in praise of the One Great Spirit, I accept this manifestation for good. I am confident it is occurring in this very moment and is everlasting. Reality is gelling right now and as the spirit of the raven(s) fly off for realms beyond, I fall into deep gratitude for this ceremony and the magical power of turning thoughts into reality.

Thank you to all the spirits and entities who attended this ceremony of power and manifestation. As I close with my sacred feather, I return blessings back to the cosmos and the One Great Spirit who makes everything work out. Blessed Be.

YELLOW RAY PLANT MAGIC

Yellow emerges from the ground and presents itself as yellow sunflowers, roses, ranunculus, daisies, pansies, begonias, black eyed Susans, dahlias, marigolds, yellow hyacinths, yellow chrysanthemums, yellow zinnia, yellow hyacinths, yellow carnations, mustards, yarrow, and lotus flowers. If you wanted to, you could have an entire garden of blooming yellow flowers. What a sight that would be first thing in the morning. Awe inspiring.

Yellow trees are eye-popping when they burst into bloom and send all of their perfume and radiance out into our world. If you've ever seen an Austrian briar, a Brazilian plume flower shrub, or a forsythia in full bloom you know exactly what I mean. Some other trees are golden trumpet, golden barbery, Japanese rose, honey perfume rose, Lydian broom, Oregon grape, palo verde, yellow trumpet, golden mimosa, Hawaiian plumeria, sweet acacia, bush cinquefoil, tipu, winter jasmine, witch hazel, yellow buckeye, yellow camellia, yellow chain, and yellow oleander. There are more trees around the world specific to their locale and weather, but most of these trees listed above can be grown in the US with additional care.

YELLOW RAY WITCHCRAFT

Other types of Witches that fall under the banner of the yellow hue are: The Correllian Witch, who practices Pagan witchcraft that includes Native American rituals. The Eclectic Witch, who can follow strict guidelines or incorporate different traditions into their practice like the Chaos Witch. The Luciferian Witch, who views Lucifer as an angel of light, questions authority, and follows a path similar to the Left-Handed Witch. The Neo-Pagan Witch, who is an umbrella witch employing the newer forms of witchcraft like Wicca or Gardnerian. And finally, the Wiccan Witch, who follows the practices created and set down by Gerald Brousseau Gardner (1884–1964) based on a reverence for nature, the practice of magic, and the worship of a goddess.

WICCA CREATIVITY SPELL

The Wicca Witch might use the qualities of the yellow ray to perform a spell for increasing creativity and awakening the dormant inner genius.

You will need:

- 2 feet of thin yellow ribbon
- 6 inches square of yellow cloth
- Lemon essential oil
- Essential oil diffuser
- Yellow candle
- 1 tsp. lemon peel
- ½ tsp yellow mustard powder
- Small piece of paper (about 3 × 3"), preferably yellow.

DIRECTIONS

Place these items on your altar. Add a few drops of lemon essential oil to the diffuser and turn it on. Light your candle. Open the yellow cloth and place the lemon peel in the center. Sprinkle the cloth with mustard powder. Add five drops of lemon essential oil to that mixture. Write an

affirmation about your creativity on your piece of paper. An example: *My ideas are as plentiful as popcorn popping in a pan on a hot stove. My creativity is as plentiful as the ocean, filled with bounty in each new wave. Thoughts and ideas are streaming to me every second, like rapid fire. There is no end to new ideas, only fresh beginnings.* Fold up your paper and add it to the packet, then tie it up with yellow ribbon. Use more ribbon to suspend the magical bag. Say:

My mind is full of creative thoughts and ideas.

My soul overflows with inspiration.

My senses are filled with fresh impressions.

My inner genius awakens and

I am flooded with insights and creativity.

In truth I speak it so. Blessed Be.

Suspend your magical pouch where you can see it, meditate, and do not block any thoughts you may have. Journal the impulses and watch what happens.

The yellow hue will always be with you. For added power, frame your art piece. At this point it is highly recommended that you take a day or two off. The yellow ray work represents a massive shift in consciousness.

MAGICAL WANDS

Another way to find the power of the yellow ray is to make a wand, if you don't already have one. I strongly recommend using a wand in your Rainbow magic, but before you choose it, you might want to take some time to understand more about the spiritual qualities of the tree it comes from. A wand made from a magical tree is a sensational item to have. Some believe that making a wand from your favorite tree—the one you have connected to the most—is the best way to go, vibrationally speaking. Others maintain procuring a wand, making it yourself, or buying it made from your birth month tree (see Appendix A on page 176) is more powerful. Others suggest that you find the qualities of the tree you like most and find a wand carved from that tree. Only you will know which wand is best for you. You will feel it in your soul.

I am asked all the time if purchasing a wand made by someone else is okay, or if it is best to make your own wand. I always respond, "You'll know." When you tap into your inner wisdom, you'll know what is best for the work you do and the life you lead, and whether or not you have any wood carving skills. There are many beautiful wands available on the Internet made by artisans who know what they are doing. There are plenty of wands to acquire and wands to dream of owning. Personally, I have an everyday wand, a crystal wand, and a formal wand with some jewels and gemstones I use for night work.

ABOUT YOUR WAND

Wands are meant for enchantment. The energy of your intention flows down your arm and into the wand. (This energy originates in your third chakra—the yellow ray propelled by the red and orange of the first and second chakras.) From the wand, that stream of intention in your mind is extended into the person, animal, or object you have selected. If you are casting a spell for prosperity for someone, form the thought and visualize them having prosperity in this moment. When you tap them with your wand, this is what is conveyed into their energy field and the cosmos. That is an example of working with a person for health.

USING A WAND FOR MAGIC

Wands have a variety of uses and are sensitive energy conductors. You can use them for casting spells, healing, enchanting objects, and summoning spirits. There are a few steps you may want to follow in preparing your wand for magical work.

1. Cleanse your wand using crystals, earth, fir needles, music, sage, cedar chips, moonlight, sunlight, or water.

2. Bring yourself into a centered state. Consecrate your wand for good magic and white lightwork.

3. Charge your wand by rubbing your hands together for 30 seconds and then placing both hands over your wand. Say "Behold, I bestow upon you my magical energy for the work we will do together. We are hereby bound together for all eternity. Amen" (Or whatever phrase you are comfortable using.)

4. Set your intention for the kind of activity you are about to commence. Say it aloud.

5. Wand etiquette. Hold your wand in your right hand for invoking, summoning, praying, or chanting. Hold the wand in your left hand when banishing or dismissing negative spirits. (If you are left hand dominant, reverse the positions.)

6. For the magical session, find a comfortable way to hold the wand in your hand or fingers. Use this as your holding position. Visualize the energy coming from your crown chakra and your heart chakra down your arm and into the wand. When you feel that charge of energy transfer to the wand, you are ready to begin.

7. Spell out your intention in the air using the wand as your pen for writing.

8. You can use your wand for spells, incantations, enchanting objects, and other magical activities. Practice the spells you know for love, career, health, money, power, happiness.

9. You can also use the wand for healing. Point the wand to the physical issue or concern without touching the area, and make circles of motion over the area while reciting a prayer, mantra, or incantation. Allow the energy to transfer from the wand to the person or animal to shower healing energy over them.

10. Never rush a spell. Allow the outcome to occur in natural time.

11. Conclude by thanking all of the entities, participants, universal energy, gods, goddesses, faeries, and nature spirits who partook in this magical session.

12. You can also clear auras, cleanse chakras, create a band of protection around yourself or someone else, and dissolve emotional blockages with your wand. Practice often and sincerely for best results.

13. Keep your wand(s) in a safe and sacred place. Cover it with a purple cloth and put it away from public contact. Recharge before your next magical session.

HEALING WITH A WAND

Using the wand to form your circle of protection and magic, make a circle in the air, create a five-dimensional orb, or draw a circle in the ground and step inside it. When you have completed your magical circle and have invited a guide or a power animal to join your ceremony, you might say something like this.

I call upon the gods and goddesses of healing. Asclepius, Greek God of Health; Sekhmet, Egyptian goddess of life and healing; Vishnu, Divine Doctor; Apollo, God of Health; or Babalú Ayé, who sees Health and Disease as One.

State the name(s) of the god or goddess you want to help and say, *I call specifically upon _____ for assistance today. Bring healing to _____ in the form of riddance and restoration. Banish the unwanted illness and restore, in its place, full and vibrant health. As I touch _____ with my wand, I send healing energy in your name into them. May the banishment begin and the quick restoration of full health follow quickly behind. In the name of all that is true and good and with gratitude to the One Great Spirit at the center of all magic and healing, I proclaim it is Done and Thus it Becomes. Blessed Be.*

The healing energy in your mind mixed with the healing energy of the entities you called forth are sent with the tap of your wand into the recipient. Make sure the energy is clear and as strong as your mental picture of them fully healed.

With a wand, you can create a circle of protection or a circle of magic. Within this circle, you will work your magic. You can also walk around your house and create a ring of protection for you and your family. Some Kitchen Witches even carve symbols and sigils on the back of their wooden spoons using a wood-burning tool so everything they cook is blessed and infused with healing energy.

Wands can be used for writing intentions in the air, drawing air symbols, enchanting the space, as well as touching or tapping an object to infuse it with the energy and mental picture you hold in your mind. Your wand is a magical pen for writing invisible words and symbols that stay present until you remove them.

Wands are used to direct your energy into the person, place, or thing you desire to help. Your job as a Rainbow Witch is to hold the picture of what you want to create as if it has already occurred and then send that energy from your mind, down through your arm, and into the object of intention.

INITIATION INTO THE YELLOW RAY

You will need to generate a sense of fun to initiate yourself into the energy of this ray. To reach its power, you'll need both a big dose of self-confidence and half a day. First, gather up your materials: a yellow outfit, jasmine incense or a yellow ray essential oil, a yellow hat, a canvas or a sheet of art paper, and four colors of paint: yellow, white, brown, and green. You will also need a brush, a yellow journal, a yellow pen, access to music (such as a phone that can play Spotify or another streaming service, a CD, or a record), a phone, a computer, a yellow bucket, and a large bouquet of yellow flowers. Note: secondhand stores can be a good source for your yellow outfit, which is a must for this exercise.

There will be three parts to this exercise with the yellow ray. Part one: grab your journal and your pen, put on your yellow outfit and your yellow hat, and take a walk. (You can bring along your phone if you want to snap photos and play music that lifts your spirits.) Walk someplace where there are stores, people, a park, or another varied environment. As you walk, make notes on everything you see that is yellow. Notice everything and everyone that passes you. If you are so inclined, snap a few shots of the things you like best. Keep walking until you find a lot of yellow images—at least thirty. Make notes on how people react to your yellow outfit. Did they smile? Did some not notice? What were the responses? How did wearing it make you feel? Note these facts neutrally, as a journalist would.

When you have gathered up your yellow research, head on home. It's now time to re-create one of the yellow images in your head, or on your camera, with your four paint colors. Before you start to paint your image, say this:

> Today I am flying free as a bird.
> I am stretching my wings
> and soaring.
>
> I'm trying new things with wild
> abandon. I am having fun being
> all that I can be.

I'm a famous painter. I call in Angel Jophiel and all my guides to help me express myself on this canvas.

I mix my colors with enlightened inspiration.

This canvas will reflect the full expression of who I am today. Blessed Be.

And now, you paint. You can use any kind of paint: acrylic, watercolor, even oil. Consider looking up online how to use your paints if this is your first time. There are so many great tutorials that will teach you the basic technique (and more, if you're interested). Lay out your paper or set up a canvas. Mix your paints: add each of the four colors to a palette or a piece of foil. The white will lighten the colors, and the brown will darken them. You can mix several variations of the same color and create an array of shades to work with. Now, paint to your heart's content in any style that moves you. That could be realistic or abstract, or you could just toss the paint at the canvas and see what happens! It's all in the spirit of great fun. Have a ball doing whatever it is you are doing. Go at it with wild abandon. When you feel that you are done, let your creation dry. Wash up, then make yourself a lemonade and wait.

When your painting has fully dried, take a good look at it in the spirit of fun. Avoid critiquing it like an art critic might—just look for what is exuberant and joyful in the image. Hold it up to the mirror and take a look at the reversal of your work, too. Hang this masterpiece in your study or private space. If ever you are ever feeling down or dispirited, have a look at the art you made and pick up on the fun that went into it. It will always be a living memory of the day you flew like a bird with the confidence of Michelangelo and the help of Archangel Jophiel.

The takeaway from this exercise is to remember that you can always create something great out of very little—you can derive joy from any resources or anything you can get your hands on, limited or otherwise. You have an invincible center filled with creative ability, and all it takes to get its power flowing again is a mild suggestion. Even Rainbow Witches have times when they feel like they can't do something or don't have what it takes. If you simply take a moment to look at your artwork and appreciate your own ability to create beauty and believe in yourself, your healing will begin instantly.

Chapter 4

THE GREEN RAY

JUNE 6–JULY 27.
THE DAY OF THE WEEK IS THURSDAY.

THE COLOR GREEN IS THE COLOR OF LIFE ON EARTH, NATURE, FRESHNESS, and fertility as well as money, finances, banking, and participating in the cycles of harmonic balance. When we tap into the powers of the green ray, we are celebrating abundance: the green of money, the green of fields, the green of new love, the color of the wind-tossed sea, the river, the color of leafy trees in spring and summer. Green calms the soul and suggests all is well, peaceful, and verdant. Green suggests a world of plenty where everyone benefits from its bounty. And at its core, this promise of the earth supplying what you need when you need it leads to green's most fundamental principle: it is the heart and the center of love in the seven rays. The theosophist Alice Bailey wrote, "Green is the basis of the activity of Nature. Green stimulates and heals. The activity system is green." What she means by this is the color green represents the manifestation of what is in the mind of creation, the results if you will, of divine thought becoming real. Love activates the intention of creation.

Love really is all there is: it is the center of life, the power, and the result of what we think and do. Love is both positive and negative; it is yin and yang; it is black and white; it is in and out; up and down; and as love is within, so it is without; it is the unseen force, and the invisible glue that holds everything together. Love has a very big job, and so do we if we are to become true Rainbow Witches. Let that love sing out loud and strong with the green ray.

Each of us carries within us enough power in the form of love to shower the world with it and in doing so raise the vibration and energy of the planet. Shakespeare said it, Einstein said it, and if we want the world to survive and thrive, we have to find pure love within ourselves and use it. If we are looking for the meaning in life, choosing love reveals the path and gives shape to our purpose.

Every word a Rainbow Witch speaks, every action a Rainbow Witch takes must come from, and be centered in, genuine love. There is no other way. Love is everywhere and in everything, and we have the opportunity to pluck it from the air, scoop it from the water, inhale it with our breath, and discover it within.

We have the green ray to illuminate the way of love, which is a gift anyone can access. Granted, there are certain times when we don't *feel* like loving someone or something. A situation can develop that challenges our feeling of love. This is precisely where the green ray triumphs.

Our feelings are like genies in bottles. Once the cork pops off, it's extremely difficult to get the genie back in or rebottle our feelings, especially if we have already expressed them. During times when people or situations cross or annoy you, they can be handled as follows, if you channel the qualities of the green ray:

When you find yourself with a disruptive person, or are in a negative situation, tap into the green ray's capacity for unconditional love. That feeling of abundance and peace will allow you to step back and play the role of a journalist. Journalists always remain neutral and objective about what they see and feel. This perspective will allow you to make kind, logical choices about what may provoke discomfort or even anger. Find ways to distance yourself emotionally by seeing what troubles you from a place of security and comfort. Disconnect from negative thoughts or feelings by changing your view. Then, take a really deep breath and release your anxieties and frustrations.

When you are tempted to meet uncomfortable circumstances with negative reactions, summon all the grace and kindness you have and ask yourself one question: *How do I want to be remembered for this moment?* When you have the answer, assume the behavior that creates your chosen result. The green ray gives us the equanimity to put thoughts before action.

In every situation we can find something in a person or a situation that stirs our sense of empathy and compassion. We can always find something good if we are willing to look deeply enough, even with the most difficult people or in the midst of challenging situations. And when things seem most challenging, say this prayer,

---

Something wonderful is happening through me right now. It's this thing called Love. Love is in my mind, Love is in my body, Love is in all my affairs. I think it. I feel it. I believe it, and I accept it. Thank you, Love.

ON YOUR ALTAR

Use the following items, or representations of those items, on your altar in order to channel the power of green ray energy.

GREEN RAY ANGEL

The archangel for the green ray is Raphael. Archangel Raphael tends to all forms of life. When you fill your sacred heart with the light that Raphael of the green ray brings you, you will never feel needy or manipulative, or require anything or anyone outside you to quench your inner longing for love. You have it all right there inside your big, beautiful heart.

Archangel Raphael is the angel of healing, first for the self and then for others he touches through you. Raphael encourages the adoration of nature, respect for all life and all beings without reservation. Raphael stands for unconditional love, and it is his joy to spread as much of that love as a person can accept. Some people only feel worthy enough to accept a thimbleful of love, but when we let the green ray infuse us, we have an unlimited capacity for love and therefore an unlimited capacity for magic. This fact alone makes it crucial that we initiate ourselves in this color ray. Green is the true ray of enlightenment.

GREEN RAY ARCHETYPE

The archetype for the green ray is the Lover. The Lover knows exactly who they are. They are filled with self-love and self-appreciation, which radiates to all beings. However, it's important to note that this archetype is balanced in love of self and others. Without first loving themselves, they could not give out as much love as they do. It's important to note that this archetype represents all aspects of love, not just romantic: friendship; maternal and paternal love; love of family; love of country; and grand, all-encompassing universal love. Knowing this and identifying with this archetype will help you expand your heart and increase your capacity to love.

GREEN RAY ASTROLOGY

The astrological sign for the green ray shares the spotlight with Libra and Aquarius: Libra for personal love and its connection to the heart chakra, and Aquarius for a more brotherly and universal love. The green ray and these signs represent both human and universal love—more like the mundane love we know and the ideal love that resides in the highest realms.

GREEN RAY FLOWER ESSENCES

If you are following Bach Flower traditions, agrimony relieves stress and anxiety and adds cheerfulness, elm helps with balance, gentian can uplift the spirit, holly helps with tolerance, honeysuckle gives relief from past loss(es), mustard is for depression relief, and rock water for increased emotional flexibility.

GREEN RAY CRYSTALS

Crystals and gemstones associated with the heart chakra include all green stones like emerald, malachite, green diamond, peridot, moldavite, jade, chrysoprase, green agate, green jasper, amazonite, chrome diopside, and many more that you can find along the way. Rose quartz, although not green, is included in the stones for this chakra.

GREEN RAY SYMBOLS

If the color green were represented by a symbol, it might be the Green Man face, the verdant countenance of Osiris the Egyptian god, a tree, a shamrock, a four-leaf clover, the goddess Venus, a cactus, a frog, an alligator, an avocado, or a Boston Celtics jersey.

GREEN RAY ESSENTIAL OILS

The essential oils designed for the heart are rose, clary sage, and rose geranium. There are grounding oils like sandalwood and patchouli, but the aromas that will lift your heart to its highest calling are the floral ones. Essential oils like cyprus and pine are also grounding. If you are suffering from loss and grief, or a broken heart, you can use frankincense, helichrysum, lavender, and sandalwood.

GREEN RAY DIVINE ENERGY

The gods and goddesses ruling this color are Airmid, the Celtic goddess of healing; Demeter, the goddess of the harvest; and Aphrodite, who ruled gardens, vegetables, and vineyards. In Roman culture, green was the color of Venus, the goddess of love.

GREEN RAY FENG SHUI

In Feng Shui practice, the color green represents the Tree or Wood element. This element is marked by the qualities of vitality, growth, rebirth, regeneration, and kindness. Wood relates to pulling nurturing ingredients up from the earth through its roots and expresses as flexibility and human openheartedness.

WORKING WITH THE GREEN RAY

For some of us, love is second nature. For others, we didn't get much of it in our formative years. The green ray offers us the chance to heal from a lack of love, and in some cases, too much love, as we can be smothered with it. With this ray we balance love, we activate love, and we use it for the purposes of creation and manifestation just like the One Great Spirit did when they had the idea of creation and loved it into reality. Some may find the green ray challenging—that's okay, keep working it and you will see how it makes more of itself once you put a little out there into the world. Balance the green ray chakra first and then evolve through the practices until love is easy for you to access and even easier for you to express.

GREEN RAY CHAKRA

The chakra of the green ray is the heart chakra, *Anahata*. Anahata is definitely the most significant chakra of the seven. Anahata is the fourth primary chakra, which lies in the middle of the other six. With three below and three above, this chakra is the bridge between the lower earth-based chakras and the upper three, which are anchored in the spiritual realm.

This chakra explores divine love and opens the energy channels of the fourth chakra by creating the energy of giving and receiving, much like the physical heart pumps blood and oxygen throughout the body supplying life to every limb and cell. The blood and oxygen circulate through the body and return to the heart for another revolution. The generous work the heart does for the body is emulated in the same give-and-take exchange of divine love in our lives. The more we receive, the more we give out; the circle thrives because of this reciprocal energy of the life force. No matter what practices you employ, making sure your heart chakra is healthy and flowing will prepare you for moving on to the next ray, the blue ray. You can always return to the green ray if you experience a loss, a tragedy, or something that affects the rhythm of reciprocal exchange within your heart and chakra system.

When the heart chakra is balanced, we are patient and honest, have open communication, and can express our emotions freely. We tend to listen well and accept input as constructive criticism to help us and support us along our path. If this chakra is imbalanced, we feel unstable, suspicious, like a martyr, repressed, unloved, lonely, jealous, and stingy. We isolate and keep things to ourselves.

This fourth chakra is critical to our life and well-being. If it is out of balance, we could end up with heart disease, lung problems, circulatory or thymus problems, allergies, asthma, immune deficiencies, and more. A Rainbow Witch really needs to keep this chakra tuned up and in balance in order to do their best work.

To recharge and clear this chakra, one of the primary therapies is to adopt or rescue a pet. They give us unconditional love that can help us to practice heart-to-heart love exchanges. If you can't have a pet of your own, then spend time visiting a friend's pet, visit shelters, volunteer, go to cat cafes to spend time with the kitties, or seek out clever ways to be close to, and in touch with, animals.

Another remedy is to get out into nature. Take a long walk, stare at the bark of a tree, roll in the grass, go barefoot. Exercise will also free the

CYMBIDIUM LOWIANUM

blockages in this chakra. Riding a bicycle is a great way to stimulate the circulation and get the juices flowing. If you happen to drive a convertible, put the top down and hit the country roads, appreciate nature, and sing at the top of your lungs. Then, get out and dance.

TREE EXERCISE FOR OPENING
THE HEART CHAKRA

I like to share this exercise with people who are struggling with blocked heart chakras. Give it a try and journal about what happens during this experience. You'll want to go into a forested area and take your journal along. Be sure to wear a green scarf or hat and tote along your green journal and green pen.

First, find a tree that speaks to you. You may want to refer back to the information on choosing a wand in the yellow ray chapter, or the list of trees and their significances in Appendix A on page 176. However, as I have mentioned, sometimes you just "know" when you've found your tree, whether or not it has magical significance. When you have found your tree and have connected, be aware of the special healing field the two of you have created together. You may want to use this field for healing on the spot. You may want to charge up healing crystals in this energy. You may want to do the same with essential oils, or talismans and amulets, or a wand. Your time with the tree is sacred and charged with energizing energy. When you part ways with the tree, you will leave with your electromagnetic energy field. The tree will remain with its field, and the third field you created together will dissipate.

Since trees are full of life and power, come to them in a spirit of respect and as often as you possibly can. You will feel enlightened and uplifted by your interaction and your heart chakra will be more open and much healthier. You may use this blessing and say it to the tree, or the souvenirs you carried home:

> May the miracles of all trees enfold you.
>
> May you find inspiration and comfort in their majesty.
>
> May their branches lift your heart upward and keep you suspended in a world of magic.

May you sense the deep, earthly connection in the mighty roots of a tree and make them your own.

May your loftiest intentions bear fruit as easily and naturally as the bounty of a tree.

May you plant your wishes in the richest soil, and, like the seeds of a tree, may they emerge effortlessly for you.

May the gentle breeze move through the branches of your mind and launch your every dream, bringing you prosperity, healing, wisdom, and love through the winds of change.

GREEN RAY DIVINATION

Green is represented in the tarot by The Empress, Justice, and Death whose meaning is change and rebirth. Consider meditating on these individual cards as you explore other methods of divination in the green ray. One that you may want to consider is automatic writing, which allows you to access your subconscious in order to gain deep wisdom.

AUTOMATIC WRITING

There is absolutely no mystery to this process, even though it may seem esoteric. It just takes a bit of skill to get into an altered state and raise your vibration high enough that "You" (meaning your ego and conscious mind) are out of the way so your higher self, other entities, or even the universe can use your hand and pen to communicate truths and meaningful messages through your body, arm, and fingers. If done correctly, you won't remember a thing *they* had you write until you come back into a mundane vibration level and read the words written in your own hand from the mind of another being and your higher self.

Sometimes the content of your writing comes directly from your own higher mind and not from outside entities. It is still important to raise your vibration in order to access the vibration of free-flowing thoughts and the wisdom that's out there. Some claim you access the Akashic Records when you elevate your consciousness to a higher rate, and the things you write about come direction from those vaults.

The experience of automatic writing is deep soul work and highly recommended for the Rainbow Witch. It's a process of opening the highways of knowledge and information to run through you today. Who knows, you might even be able to access a time when you were in another civilization, in another time. Here are the steps you will need to take before beginning automatic writing.

In order to start, you'll need pen and paper. (No laptops please.) This information must come through your own body to be of importance and authenticity.

Naturally, you'll need a quiet space where you can be undisturbed. Then you'll need time to clear your mind. You may want to light a candle and diffuse an essential oil like lavender, Melissa, or yuzu. Preprogram a quartz crystal with the intention of connecting with your highest self and guides. Keep it nearby. Breathe deeply until your muscles are relaxed. Start sending your breath to the top of your head and work down, imagining

9-STEP RITUAL FOR GREEN WITCHES TO ASSESS HEART MAGIC IN A TREE

1. Find a tree that appeals to you from the heart. Stand beside it. Ask the tree for its permission to connect. Ask it if it will share its essence with you. Be sure to confirm that you mean no harm. Find something from the tree that has fallen—a leaf, a piece of bark, a seed, a cone, a branch, a twig—and take it into your hands. Close your eyes and concentrate deeply on what you have picked up. Feel the texture, experience the weight, note the temperature. Does it speak to you in some way? Can you feel the life in it? Does it have a scent?

2. Open your eyes after connecting with the piece of the tree. Observe the entire tree. Walk around it. Look into the ground to visualize the roots. Try to sense its aroma. Observe the bark. Gaze intently at the leaves, twigs, needles, branches. Is the tree symmetrical, asymmetrical, twisted, straight, gnarled? Now, pay attention to the colors in all the parts of the tree, honoring each one you see as colors of the rainbow. In your mind, label the colors: use colorful adjectives, and try to describe the tree in as many poetic terms as you can.

3. When you have a picture of the tree clearly in your mind, close your eyes and re-create the tree in your imagination. Begin to feel the tree's inner life. Don't open your eyes yet. Answer these questions: Is the tree male or female or other in your feelings? What element comes to mind when you tune into the kinesthetics of the tree? What else can you sense about the tree? When you visualize the tree, do you hear music? Birds? Other sounds?

4. Once you have catalogued the tree's qualities in your mind, you may open your eyes and begin to write them down in your green ray journal. At this point you may want to engage in a spoken dialogue with the tree. Say something like, "I'm sensing that your talent and magic is protection, would that be correct?" or "I'm feeling you have a nurturing spirit? Am I on the right track?" "Are you able to communicate with the fairies? The other world?" "Is there a spirit that lives within you?" "May I please know their name(s)?" "Are you a tree of love?" "Can your magic bring long life?" "Would you say you are a tree of good fortune?" "Does your magic purify and cleanse?"

Keep asking positive questions until you get a sense of what the tree's purpose is and what it enjoys doing. If you remain open and in this meditative state, the tree will give you the answers.

5. At the end of your conversation with the tree, ask it how you can be of service to it. I like to ask if there is anything it is afraid of. Once a tree told me, "Rodents," so I wrapped a slick tube of aluminum around the trunk that the rodents couldn't climb. It seemed to be much happier and produced a wonderful crop of fruit that year.

6. You might consider a few other methods of achieving closeness with your tree. I often tell the tree about all of the good things that are being done in the world to help trees. I bring a bag of nutrients for a tree if it is fading and, once in a while, if I revisit the tree, I might tell it about the products that we make from it (bark, medicine, seeds, needles, wood, roots) and how they help people. Trees love it when you chat with them. You could even sing songs for the tree if you are so inclined, or bring a gift that your tree might enjoy. Some suggestions: tobacco as a token of the earth, crystals or stones from the ground,

or even a sack full of ladybugs that can assist in warding off other insects that might plague your tree.

7. Before you leave, spend time thanking the tree. Ask it if you may have some of its products, such as leaves, needles, cones, or branches. Most often the answer is yes, but if the tree says "no," let it be. There may be something going on you don't understand. Trust that you will know exactly what to do. If you want to take a photo, be sure to ask for permission to take a photo or sketch the tree and be sure to make sure the tree is compensated for the time it spends with you in the form of gratitude and little gifts.

8. Take your time making notes, so you don't forget what you discussed with the tree. Ask the tree if you can return again. You may want to say the blessing for a tree at the end of this chapter.

9. When you return home, find a special and sacred place to set your tree souvenirs. Let them remind you of the precious time you spent with them, the connection you had, and the confirmation of questions asked and answered, so you can cherish a deeper sense of what gifts the tree holds.

that warm honey is being poured over you. Relax little by little as the imaginary honey reaches the floor. When you are relaxed, pick up your pen and place it on the paper. Force nothing. Breathe freely. Have a relaxed grip on your pen. Relax your hand. Now, wait.

You may begin to feel movement. Keep your eyes closed and allow it. Keep breathing. Stay in this space for at least twenty minutes. Bring yourself out of the trance slowly and gently. When it feels right, open your eyes. Your page may have lettering, or it may have symbols, pictures, or squiggles. Remember, this is your first attempt. Whatever happened, don't attach any judgment, whether positive or negative. Let it be.

If you want to try it again, repeat the same steps and see what happens. Some people will take to this like snow to a mountaintop, and others will find the process isn't suited to them. Give it a try. Whatever the results, you will have learned something, and that alone is valuable. You may also discover you have a real talent for this practice. You may be able to access not only your higher self, but the higher selves for others, as well.

You'll never know until you give it a try. As the Brits say, "Keep calm and carry on." When you are trying new practices like this one under the banner of the green ray, all you need to remember is that it all comes from the heart.

GREEN RAY PLANT MAGIC

The flowers of the green ray are the button flower, Anastasia spider mum, bells of Ireland, green cymbidium orchid, anthurium, and stinking hellebore.

If you want a green tree, you pretty much have your pick of the litter; some trees with green flowers are the evergreen amaryllis, green ball sweet William, green jewel coneflower, green star sword lily, greenspire hydrangea, lime green flowering tobacco, Francisca polyanthus primrose, Benary's giant lime zinnia, green goddess calla lily, and HGC green Corsican Lenten rose.

GREEN RAY MAGICAL BIRD

Peacocks are birds of mystery in that they look small and humble, until they open their tail feathers and dazzle the world. In that instant, they rule with their magic. For self-protection, a peacock can crowd into a small space and only show themselves when they choose to. They represent the green ray in their display of shimmering colors and the manner in which they share their beauty with the world. We can never hide what is in our hearts forever, and the peacock reminds us that we have to spread out our feathers and shine, proudly and confidently, to truly live and thrive. When we display our true colors, we are authentically claiming our place in the world.

The peacock is a symbol of reinvention, royalty,

beauty, and protection. Their scream can ward off intruders. In ancient Egypt, the eyes of the peacock were said to be like the Eye of Horus. The peacock also reawakens our sense of beauty and offers a fresh perspective with their transformational talents. Ancient shamans taught that peacocks possess extraordinary healing powers, like the way an act of forgiveness can transform a heart.

Peacocks represent the natural world hosting the colors of a garden in their feathers. There is nothing more grand, imperial, and elegant than a peacock in full display.

PEACOCK CEREMONY FOR HEALING AND TRANSFORMATION

You will need:

- Three peacock feathers, or feathers painted to match the pattern of a peacock

- A piece of peacock ore (a rough stone with iridescent metallic colors) placed in a fireproof bowl

- Matches

- Pen and magic wish or flying paper to write on

- Rose essential oil and diffuser

Each peacock feather represents the past, the present, and the future. Start your diffuser with the rose essential oil. Remove the peacock ore you have placed in the bowl. Set aside three pieces of magic flying wish paper. Write on one piece of paper what is in the past that you want changed or healed. Write on another one what obstacle is presently blocking your healing or transformation. Write on the third how happy you will look and feel in the future when this transformation/healing has occurred. Place all three pieces of paper in the bowl. Wave the three peacock feathers over the bowl three times and say:

> Glimmering sight of kaleidoscope tail,
> Unfurled in wind, a halyard sail
> All can see your bold display,
> And bow their heads for royalty.
> Praise be given for favors asked,
> The past unfolds, the future's masked
> In present now, before our eyes
> Clean the plate of evil passed
> Transform the now, remove the mask
> So futures bright may last and last.

Light the papers in the burning bowl.

> Open wide the panoply.
> The deed is done and now we're free.
> Of the past and of the crushing weight
> The future's come, let's celebrate.

To close the ritual, place the peacock ore back in the bowl. Turn off the diffuser and close your ceremony by thanking all participants.

GREEN RAY WITCHCRAFT

Many other types of witches fall under the ray of the green ray: The Axis Mundi Witch believes in a central pillar that connects heaven and earth.

The Celtic Witch emphasizes Celtic deities, mythology, and rituals, and practices earthcentric magic. The Cottage Witch is focused on their home and includes some practices from the Green and Kitchen Witch practices. The Faery Witch works with the fae and is grounded in Scottish and Celtic practices and beliefs. The Green Witch is deeply connected to the earth and is frequently called a Forest Witch. Finally, the Hearth Witch is part herbal and part magic, heals with both, and shares a similarity with the Kitchen Witch because they usually practice at home.

CELTIC WITCH GREEN RAY RITUAL

A Celtic Witch might activate the green ray by working with the goddess Airmed for healing and protection. Draw your circle of love, select your tools, green candle, green stone like a piece of Presli bluestone from Stonehenge, and green essential oil like clary sage or rose geranium, diffused. Light your green candle, and send out grace, goodness, and blessings to the person or situation. Send love, even when it feels difficult to do so. Invite your guides and master teachers to join you in the ritual. You might want to use a prayer like this:

> May I be happy, May I be healthy, May I be safe, May I live with ease.

Visualize the person or situation and repeat:

> May you be happy, May you be healthy, May you be safe, May you live with ease.

Then picture the conflict resolved and say:

> May we be happy, May we be healthy, May we be safe, May we live with ease. I proclaim peace in the world, peace

in my heart, peace in your heart, and peace to all living beings. May all the world live in peace.

Add in anything else you want to say to personalize this blessing and end with thanking your guides and masters and conclude with *Blessed Be.* Thank the entities and the goddess Airmed for being with you and sending out love for you.

INITIATION INTO THE GREEN RAY

Find a green journal and a green pen. On the first page, draw a heart that is approximately five inches high. Enter the answers to the following twenty questions on a scale of 1–10, where 1 means strongly disagree and 10 means strongly agree. Write the numbers inside the heart.

SCORES

If you scored above 150, your heart chakra is open and flowing. You are already aligned with the energy of the green ray, but make a note of the areas where you may need to place your attention for improvement.

If your score was 100–150, this is a reminder that there are areas where you may need to do some work in forgiveness, trust, and self-love.

If you score below 100, this is a flashing yellow light for you. Before you step into the green ray and work with its power, you will need to address some issues within yourself. There are blockages within your heart chakra, and now is the time for you to do some work to open them up. Reread the questions, pinpoint the areas where you scored the lowest, and begin there, one step at a time. You can take this test as often as you like to see how open your heart chakra is or is becoming. Refer back to the Green Ray Chakra section to find some exercises for activating this part of yourself before you move on.

Answer these questions.

1. Are you able to let go of something or a situation easily?
2. If someone wrongs you, are you able to forgive them?
3. How would you rate yourself on the jealousy scale?
4. Do you hold grudges?
5. Do you tend to be bitter about an experience?
6. Do you believe love can heal all things?
7. Do you reach out to people when you are sad and lonely?
8. Do you put others first and yourself last?
9. Do you believe you have a right to be loved?
10. How compassionate are you?
11. Do you like to volunteer and help causes?
12. Have you experienced a big loss in your life?
13. Were you able to release your sorrow?
14. Do you love your work?
15. Does your head rule your decisions?
16. Do you follow your heart in matters?
17. How easy is it for you to give and receive love?
18. Do you believe you are loveable?
19. Can you love yourself just as you are?
20. How important is being loved to you?

When you have answered all twenty questions and have assigned number values to each inside the heart, add up your score. This exercise is an indicator of how balanced you are in your heart chakra. Never be disheartened; not even the saints could score a perfect 200.

1.
2.
3.
4.
5.
6.
7.
8.
9.
10
11.
12.
13.
14.
15.
16.
17.
18.
19.
20.

Chapter 5

THE BLUE RAY

JULY 28–SEPTEMBER 19.
THE DAY OF THE WEEK IS FRIDAY.

WHEN A TELEVISION STATION HIRES AN ART DIRECTOR TO DESIGN ITS news set, the art director asks the station manager, "What color of blue do you want?" This is because the art director knows that blue is the color of truth: it brings about serenity, calmness, and reliability, no matter what the TV anchor is reporting.

Blue can also be a color of authority and honor. When you win first prize for your pie at the county fair, or your horse wins by a nose length at the Kentucky Derby, they pin a blue ribbon on the winner. Blue is often equated with uniforms, such as the police or military. Since the color blue symbolizes harmony, it was the color chosen for the United Nations flag.

On the flip side, blue is also associated with despair and depression: when your sweetheart leaves you and breaks your heart, you can have a bad case of the *blues*. Billie Holiday sang the blues. And Elvis danced in his blue suede shoes, but how do you think Picasso felt during his *blue period?*

On the surface, blue may appear to be a simple classification, but don't let it fool you. The color blue and the blue ray have many layers. Doctors know that the color blue can lower a pulse rate and body temperature. How many blue foods can you name? Blueberries would be right at the top of the list and perhaps plums, but most food is considered rotten if it is blue, case in point, blue cheese.

The language of blue is fascinating. On one hand a blue moon is a prophetic thing because it means you have a full moon twice in the same month, like a bonus. On the other hand, having the blues is a bit of a drag. Blue Monday is alleged to be the worst and most depressing day of the year.

Blue is the color of sincerity, and calms like twilight, the sky, a placid ocean, and generally elicit feelings of happiness from people. Blue is calming because many people feel comfortable in their own skin when they're in the presence of the color blue. Nerves are calmed and channels of communication are opened and encouraged by blue.

Green or blue is chosen for surgical scrubs because the colors are the opposite of the red spectrum. This means that the surgeon can be singularly focused on the red colors of the organs and vital fluids and not be distracted by nuances or colors in the environment. This improves the likelihood of a better outcome for patient and doctor alike. Alice Bailey believed that blue was the color that "represents as much of the solar quality to which humanity can respond." For her, the sun represented all the power in the cosmos. The energies of blue were so special to her that she created the first New Age logo and used blue as the dominant color.

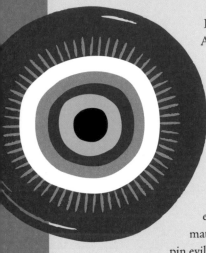

Internationally, blue has different meanings. In Afghanistan, Turkey, Greece, and other Balkan countries, blue amulets worn by a person are thought to ward off evil. You may be familiar with the evil eye of Greece.

The Greeks believe a mati carries a curse from the person who gives it to you. If you receive an evil eye, you might find yourself weak, suffering from headaches, confused, tense, exhausted, or the recipient of bad luck. The way the Greeks think is to fight evil with evil and protect yourself against the curse of the mati using the mati. For protection, Greek mothers pin evil eye beads to the clothing of their children, many adults wear a mati necklace or amulet. Some hang them in the entrance to their homes, and some paint the mati on their exterior walls. The mati is usually blue because it represents the color of non-Greek-colored eyes (blue) that may bring evil and place curses on them. This belief dates back to the sixth century BCE.

According to Greek custom, protection against the evil eyes comes in the form of wearing one, or by performing a *xematiasma*, which is Greek for "an undoing of the eye." Negative energy, like jealousy, anger, or hostility creates the evil eye. The ceremony has prayers attached which are handed down, men to women and women to men generationally. If a woman teaches a woman, or a man teaches a man, the prayers will not work. At my home I have a mati at the front door and a mati in the backyard. Often, I wear a mati bracelet, right next to my bracelet made from the bluestone of Stonehenge, but for different reasons than you may think.

A Rainbow Witch chooses not to engage in this age-old superstition, but sees the mati, or *evil eye*, as something wonderful, positive, and a reminder of our universal oneness. Collectively, we have one eye, one mind, one nose, one mouth, one heart, and one consciousness. That's the concept we now attach to the mati. If you choose to use the mati as a symbol of oneness, as I do, put it at your front door as a welcome that silently exudes the feeling, "Welcome, we recognize all are one." Placed anywhere around your home or yard, it can reinforce the same message to the trees, plants, neighbors, animals domestic and otherwise, to let nature clearly know you believe you are one with all of it.

ON YOUR ALTAR

Use these items and representations of the concepts below to add blue ray energy to your altar. Add blue stones, crystals, candles, and flowers if you like to honor the blue ray.

BLUE RAY ANGEL

The archangel for the blue ray is Michael. Archangel Michael is the supreme commander of all the heavenly forces of angels and archangels. He triumphs over enemies in the fight for truth and justice. He is also known for his healing properties. Constantine the Great built a sanctuary to Archangel Michael called *Michaleon*, which was built on the site of a Pagan temple associated with medicine and reputed for its healing waters. Christians came from far and wide to indulge in the curative, healing waters.

Archangel Michael brings us grace to help us speak with kind words, and for releasing judgment, criticism, and damaging thoughts and actions. He encourages us to battle for the truth and be righteous in our thoughts and actions. He reminds us that taking without giving depletes us and that reciprocal giving back completes the circle and keeps us whole. He encourages us to use our ability to communicate in order to spread joy, wise counsel, and truth instead of lies and slander.

BLUE RAY ASTROLOGY AND COSMOLOGY

The planetary ruler of the blue ray is Saturn. It is the planet that makes us feel one with the cosmos, nature, and other living things. Saturn also brings us the tests in life to measure our sense of right and wrong and our truth and integrity. It is the planet of morals and justice. Saturn is like a good judge who brings fairness to our lives as long as there is discipline and hard work. The trials Saturn dishes out are always for the betterment of the person. Saturn is the planet of karma giving back what a person serves up.

If you're looking for a blue star in the sky, find the constellation of Orion and you'll see Rigel, the brightest star in the constellation, and the sixth brightest star in the sky. Interestingly, Rigel is 700–900 light-years away from earth, yet it burns as bright as Sirius which is 8.3 light-years away. Here's another mind-shaking fact, Rigel puts out 40,000 times the energy of the sun. That's a ton of power. Another amazing blue star is Eta Carinae, 8,000 light-years away, which lives in the Carina constellation. Eta Carinae gives off five million times more the energy than the sun. If these stars were closer, we'd all burn up instantaneously. Eta Carinae gives off radiation in the ultraviolet spectrum, which human eyes cannot perceive. Human eyes see it as blue light, but hummingbirds and bees can see the full ultraviolet spectrum.

BLUE RAY ARCHETYPE

The archetype for the blue ray is the Communicator, who understands the power of words because they represent the thoughts, beliefs, and feelings of a person. These words can be clear, truthful, and helpful, or they can be hurtful, deceptive, manipulative, and false. The higher gift of the archetype is to be a channel for good, clarity, unity, and growth. The lower aspect of the archetype is critical, damning, blameful, and selfish. The blue ray follows the green ray, making it full of love and ready to speak the truth.

BLUE RAY FLOWER ESSENCES

The Bach Flowers that are related to the color blue and the fifth chakra are holly for trust and acceptance of others, white chestnut for discernment and mental balance, wild oat for feelings of fulfillment and belonging, and agrimony for a joyful attitude. All of these help with focus, emotional positivity, and building trust. These essences will help you remain in the truth and speak from your heart.

BLUE RAY CRYSTALS

Stones for the blue ray can be blue apatite, blue calcite, lapis lazuli, kyanite, aventurine, azurite, rhodusite, shattuckite, sodalite, blue lace agate, angelite, larimar tourmaline, and aquamarine. You also may find others that fall in the blue ray hue.

BLUE RAY SYMBOLS

If you are working with the blue ray and wish to add a visualization of its energy to your altar, look for a symbol of trust, friendship, unity, and loyalty. In Asia, two golden fish side by side symbolize the trust a couple has in assuming a comingled life to take on trials together. The knot is a symbol of trust across many cultures. In Ireland, the claddagh, two hands holding a heart, serves a similar purpose. Bamboo is a great representation of blue ray energy, indicating unity. Because the roots grow together and become entangled, this plant symbolizes our connection to each other, family, and the worldwide community.

BLUE RAY ESSENTIAL OILS

Essential oils compatible with the blue ray are lavender, blue chamomile, blue yarrow, blueberry, and blue tansy. (Note: blue tansy is nontoxic, but tansy oil contains thujone, which is poisonous.)

BLUE RAY DIVINE ENERGY

The gods and goddesses in the blue ray are Panchavaktra shiva, from India with five heads and four arms, and the Shakti represents the fifth chakra. Lord Krishna is depicted having blue skin, Athena had eyes that were as blue as the sky, Poseidon ruled the blue sea, Aphrodite, was the daughter of the sea, and Ether, Uranus, and Zeus all fall under the blue ray.

BLUE RAY FENG SHUI

In Feng Shui, blue represents water. Water always seeks its lowest point and cannot contain itself but relies on a physical boundary to act as its sides and bottom. Water requires containment, or it would dissipate and be lost. Water can be destructive as well as life-giving. A tidal wave can easily destroy an unsuspecting village, yet a sip of water can bring life back to a dehydrated traveler.

WORKING WITH THE BLUE RAY

Try the practices below to work with the power of the blue ray.

BLUE RAY SPELL

Sigils are perfect ways to express your emotions, connect with your intuition, and expand your effectiveness, using the qualities connected with the blue ray. Sigil magic is another way to use symbols in your spells. One of the most powerful tools a Rainbow Witch can have in their skill set is Sigil Magic. We see sigils all around us. Billboards are sigils, logos for corporate brands are sigils. The sign above your local gas station is a sigil. Sigils are symbolic and visual representations of an idea, concept, or meaning to the subconscious. The reason they are so powerful is that many of them represent universal meaning and result in emotion and feeling. Sigils are used to incite emotion, elicit action, or create transformation.

For example, when our human minds see a symbol like skull and crossbones on a bottle of cleaner, we know it means "poison." The skull registers as death and the crossbones suggest "don't get involved with this or you could end up like the skeleton shown here." In this case, the image is helpful and potentially lifesaving.

There are variations on the concept of sigils throughout different cultures. In Voodoo they use *Veves* for casting spells, symbols that call in prosperity and keep evil away. Almost every religion is indelibly associated with its symbols—Christianity with the cross, Judaism with the Star of David, for example. When you think about it, sigils are all over the place.

In making your own sigils you imbue them with magic and intention and send them into your subconscious to elicit action or change. You become the creator of these shortcuts to the subconscious, which is the seat of all change, transformation and fulfillment, and the instigator of powerful magic in motion.

Sigils are magical mechanisms for fulfilling your dreams and desires. They require preparation in the form of clarity, self-knowledge, and time. You should not make a sigil if you are angry, upset, stressed, or wishing evil for someone else.

You also need to know how to write a statement that is affirmative and descriptive for your desires. On a personal note, if you are a visual person like I am, then sigils will definitely speak to you and make your magical work much more powerful. You don't have to be a visual person to appreciate sigils. They work for all of us no matter our approaches.

MAKING YOUR PERSONAL SIGIL FOR THE RAINBOW AND SIGIL WITCH

The first thing to do in order to create a sigil is to engage in a calming technique. You must enter into this work with a clear mind and a calm heart. Find a private, solitary place that is quiet and calm. Meditate, chant, or otherwise center yourself however you choose. Burn a candle, light some incense, diffuse essential oils, play music, and allow stillness to wash over you before you begin this sacred work. Take your time clearing out the stresses of the day and your worries about the future and use your practice to be completely present in the moment. It is essential that you ready your inner magician for this work.

If you any have doubt in your mind that sigils work, then the first two sigils you should make are "Sigils work" and "My sigils are effective." We must educate our subconscious to follow our desires. Doing this action clears away any resistance we may have to attaining our stated goals. We never know what disbeliefs are lurking in the subconscious.

You need to craft a statement for your sigil that communicates what you want. If you want a new home and a garden, your statement might be something like "My new house is spacious, with a fertile garden." If you want a romantic relationship, you might say "My new mate is kind, loving, sharing, employed, and loves children." Or "Perfect love and a lasting relationship come to me easily." For more money, "Prosperity fills my heart and my bank account." For health, "My body and mind are perfect and healthy." For a new job, "I am blessed with a perfect job and ample pay."

For general desires you can use phrases and statements like "Goodness and kindness fill my heart and life." "I release anything negative in my life that does not serve my purpose." "Love and beauty fill my days." "I forgive and release _____." "I am grateful for _____ in my life and thank them for the lessons they provide(d)." Some of those statements are longer than they need to be, but you will have an opportunity later on to shorten them.

Step three is to write down what you want to achieve. If you need a quick refresher, do this: make a list of all the good things you have ever attracted into your life. Then, make a list of all of the not-so-good things you have attracted into your life. The reminder here is that we are responsible for co-creating both the positive and negative things in our lives, so take credit for the good and make notes of the not-so-desirable. Be sure you don't use words like *should, don't,* and *must,* in your list. Stay free of making commands or using any terms that reprimand or scold yourself. Exchange the word *could* for *should* or *ought to.* Keep it all possible and positive.

After you do that, make a list of the things you want to create in your life. Include the things you want to change or invite in. This step is not like the list above. This is about taking the helm and supporting your desires with the action of co-creation. Sigils are all about co-creation. Keep reading.

In the next list, make a note of how your life would change if everything you want came true. Describe what your life would be like if you already had those improvements. Now add a feeling(s) for each accomplishment. Tell us how you would feel if you had these dreams come true. Take your time. This is an extremely important step. When you finish that list, complete with emotions, make a final list of what actions you could take to achieve those results. Allow your inner creative genius to sprout. Consider several approaches you might take to help make your desires come true. They don't even have to be in the realm of possibility. The idea is to stimulate your creative juices and get your brain going to find a solution even if it doesn't seem possible. Judge nothing. Just let your creativity bubble up and overflow. What you might discover is that in your wildest thinking there is a pathway you would never have thought about taking otherwise.

Finally, when you have all of your lists made, write down this phrase on your list of desired changes: "or in any way the universe chooses to fulfill it for my highest good." Don't forget this step. Remember, we never tell the powers of the universe *how* to accomplish the task; we want to give it full freedom to do what's best for us.

Here is the process of making a sigil that has the power to influence the subconscious:

+ First, create your statement (intention) using positive language. Think about what you want, what difference it will make in your life if you get it, how you will feel about it when you get it, ways in which you might be able to get it, who might help you, where you might begin, and what is holding you back. Think upon those things as you craft your statement. When you've had a good think about the parameters, construct your statement and affirmative intention. Write it out in capital letters.

- Then, remove all the vowels. You can just cross them out and the rewrite the statement in caps without the vowels.

- After that, remove all duplicate letters and recopy your statement in capitals.

- Create *chaos* by recopying all the letters in caps in a random way on a sheet of paper.

- In this step, you're going to rewrite all the letters again, in any random fashion, but make sure they touch each other. Repeat this step until you have an image you like. This is the fun part: playing with the arrangement of the letters until you find one you love.

- Once you have the image you like, enclose it in a circle or a square shape to seal it. You now have a sigil for your intention and desire.

When you create your sigil, you can use any medium you like, such as colored pens, pencils, felt markers, or paintbrushes. You can also use different materials like felt, papyrus, and colored paper. Be as artistic as you like with your lettering. You can incorporate photographs, rocks, wood, fabric, canvas, or any other materials you fancy. Once you have finished your work of art, then you must *activate* it.

The next step is to charge your sigils. This step strengthens the sigil's silent power. It is also a good practice to anoint it by using items that coincide with your birth date and month. You can charge your sigil using Reiki, sunlight, moonlight, music, the smoke from smudging, or by performing a ritual you create for amplifying sigil power.

Now, repeat the original phrase you wrote down three times while holding your hands over the sigil. Conclude by adding the phrase *or in any way the universe chooses to fulfill it for my highest good.*

This is the step where you want to impress upon your brain this wondrous sigil image you have created and then, as an act of faith in the universe, destroy it. This practice is much like one performed by Buddhist monks, who, after they work on a large sand painting for days and days, mess it all up and give away small jars of sand to those who watched them work as a symbol of natural change, as well as faith in the fact that another painting can be created.

To achieve the full imprint and complete the destroy (release) phase, stare at your sigil for five minutes. You can gaze at it longer if you wish, depending on your personal practice. Five minutes sets the imprint into your brain. Now, you need to destroy it. This action demonstrates faith in the universal order of things.

You can burn it safely or fold it up and send it out to sea in a tiny boat. You can toss it into the wind from a high perch, you can write it in the air, or you can draw it in the sand or snow and let nature take it away.

If you absolutely cannot part with your sigil, then you are also free to display it in a place where your subconscious can see it frequently. If you have created a work of art with your design, you may want to frame it and hang it in a location of honor. I've also seen witches make their sigils into jewelry, tattoo them on their bodies, and turn them into postcards and mail those postcards out to friends. There is no end to the creativity you will have with your sigil. Your sigil remains charged and is reactivated and recharged every time someone views it.

Some places where you can display you sigil might be at the front door or entryway, if you are making a sigil for harmony or protection; a specific room in your home where you will see it often; as a bumper sticker, if you are wanting peace in the world; on clothing, bags, gift wrap, return address stickers, seals, logos, signs in the garden, rugs, or furniture. I like to place mine near my collection of tower crystals for extra activating power.

The biggest question I am asked is, "How will I know my sigil is working?" We all want to know that, don't we? The answer is twofold, and you'll know it when you see the results. Remember, the One Great Spirit doesn't wear a watch. If you see no results, then you will wait at least three months and revisit your original intention. You may want to get some help or input on the way it is written. Rewrite your original in three or four different versions until you make sure it is completely a positive expression and uses a statement that you have already achieved the goal. For example, if you want to be rid of annoying headaches and you have written, "I no longer have headaches," rewrite it to read, "My head is clear, bright, and pain-free." If you are wanting to lose weight and have written, "I need to stop eating cookies," rewrite it to read, "My body is healthy and vibrant in every moment." If you've written, "I want peace in the world," rewrite it to say, "The world is peaceful and free."

Don't overthink your sigil. Sometimes it takes practice to get the process right. Be patient with yourself and reach out for help if you need it. Follow the directions, write the statement, remove the vowels, excise duplicate letters, and redraw your remaining letters into a design where all letters touch on one side. Charge it up, bless it, stare at it for five minutes, and then let it go. Then all you have to do is wait for the manifestation to occur.

There is a lot written about the children of the blue ray. They are not what some people call "indigo children," but they have some similarities. Blue ray children are born intuitive, they are anchored in healing and making the world a better place. They are extremely sensitive to the world around them, and they can see things many others cannot. They are temperamental at times, but you can recognize them by their affinity for water. They need to be by a lake, the ocean, a river, a stream, or even in a pool as often as possible.

Blue ray children have uncommonly close connections to animals. They can construct a make-believe world in minutes with their fertile imaginations. They are sensitive, able to read feelings, and are perceptive, passionate, confident, creative, and self-assured. They are the future. Nurture them. And if you recognize these qualities in yourself, it is right that you are becoming a Rainbow Witch. If you are or were once a blue ray child, you're already partway there.

Lastly, I want to share with you the Rainbow Witch Promise for creating and using sigils.

One. The intention behind your sigil must be benevolent and helpful to people and animals and the planet

Two. You must never create a sigil to control the lives or free will of another.

Three. Do not create sigils to activate the subconscious of others for material gain (for example to purchase items from you or your website).

Four. Don't use sigils to claim specific powers for yourself that serve only your ego or wallet.

Five. Never use sigils to influence anyone to give you money, hire you, or fall in love with you.

If you agree with these, please say, out loud, "I agree."

Sigils are simple and powerful devices for transforming your own mind by changing your beliefs. Think about what the sigils like the runes or the Ogham have done for the Norse and the Celts. They are powerful tools. Creating your own sigils gives you a similar utility, and perhaps if you hone your craft, the symbols you will make—or at least the intention behind them—will have a long-lasting and powerful effect.

BLUE RAY DIVINATION

The tarot cards of the blue ray are The High Priestess, The Hanged Man, and Temperance. These are powerful cards with important meanings: The High Priestess is associated with secrets and inner knowledge—waiting for the universe to give you your answers rather than chasing them with knowledge and conscious thought. The High Priestess asks you to follow your intuition to what you desire. Likewise, The Hanged Man denotes a period of reflection and waiting, which can lead to wisdom. And Temperance is a card of balance, moderation, and patience, which, likewise, can lead to greater knowledge.

BLUE RAY CHAKRA

As we have mentioned before, blue is the color of the fifth chakra, *Vishuddha*, which means "purifying mind and body." Blue is the sky, the ocean, representing open spaces, a sense of freedom, expansiveness, imagination, and intuition. Blue for many cultures is associated with royalty, the military, trust, loyalty, business, and nature.

The benefits of working to balance the fifth chakra are critical to living a life connected to your higher chakras and acting as a guardian for your lower ones. Being able to live in truth, and from truth, is the measure of a powerful person.

BLUE RAY PLANT MAGIC

Blue flowers are stunning in a garden. Some varieties are the blue nasturtium, phacelia, California bluebell, cosmos, cornflower, hydrangea, salvia, lily of the Nile, rose of Sharon, iris, lobelia, gentian, brunnera, globe thistle, delphinium, false indigo, bluebeard, big blue sea holly, blue penstamon, Virginia bluebells, bellflower, aster, spike speedwell, and Felicia daisy.

If it's a blue ray tree you want, look for the blue jacaranda, blue wisteria, rose of Sharon, blue butterfly bush, blue rhododendrons, lignum vitae, crepe myrtle, fragrant lilac, and the Texas mountain laurel.

BLUE RAY MAGICAL BIRD

The Roc is another amazing, legendary bird who was said to have had a wingspan of forty-eight feet. It is said the Roc looked like a giant eagle with enormous talons. This gigantic bird picked up the shipwrecked Sinbad and intended to take him high up in the sky to its nest. To escape the nest, Sinbad ingeniously tied himself to the Roc's leg with his turban and landed on earth unharmed.

The Roc is tied to the blue ray's qualities of communication, magic, and healing. This creature also represents self-rescue and how we can save ourselves when we need to. Because the wingspan of the Roc is so enormous, it was said the bird caused an eclipse when it flew in front of the sun. Having the power to occlude the light is a way of forcing a change of focus by taking light off the subject we are engaged with, and which may be obscuring our karmic path. Like Sinbad, sometimes we must undertake imaginative measures to save ourselves.

When you feel at the end of your rope, like you are going to explode or a situation seems like it is out of control, call upon the Roc for help. With her giant wings, she can get to you within seconds.

ROC SPELL FOR CHANGE

Use an eagle feather or paint another bird feather to look like an eagle's. During this spell, a figurine of a Roc, or at least a picture of the bird, is a wonderful thing to have on your altar. She represents power and change; dramatically leaving one path and going to another with might.

Take the feather in your dominant hand and a stone of your choice (a sunstone is good for strength) in your non-dominant hand. Perform your favorite grounding exercise. Raise your arms to the sky, and proclaim, *Oh Mighty and Beneficent Roc, come to me and show me the way out. Guide me to my next destination and extract me from my present situation.*

Stand strong, wait for the whoosh and the uplift. When you feel it, you'll know change is afoot.

Proclaim what you want to be rescued from. Say it loud and with force. *Take me now mighty Roc, carry me swiftly away with your love and* compassion. *Bring me to the next step, a level up, and do it now. For my highest good may we now depart.*

Go deep within as you wait for a shift. Listen for it. Feel it. Release yourself from the grip of the talons. Softly let that release take you gently to your knees.

It is done. I am transported into my next phase. The past is dissolved, and I am free of it. No person, place, or thing has power over me now. I am rescued. I feel it in my marrow. It is a brand-new day and I face it with power and gratitude for the help of the Roc when I needed it most. I am wholly revived and filled with the power of the sun. I can do anything now, and I will. All hail the mighty Roc. I release you, Roc, to assist another. Thank you and fly with my love and gratitude, Blessed Be.

BLUE RAY WITCHCRAFT

The Witches falling under the blue ray are:
The British Traditional Witch, who practices with the superstitions and spells from the British Isles. The Egyptian Witch, who focuses on the Egyptian Deities and magic. The Elemental Witch, who works with the five elements of earth, water, fire, air, and spirit. The Folk Witch, who follows a

similar path to British witchcraft using their magic for practical purposes and passed down through generations, also known as "cunning folk" or wise people. The Music Witch, who uses the magic and mystery of music as the basis of their practice. The Sea Witch, who has strong ties to water, especially the ocean and uses gifts from the ocean and beach in their practice. And finally, the Sigil Witch, also known as a "word witch," who uses sigils and words throughout their magic.

INITIATION INTO THE BLUE RAY

Staying loyal to your beliefs and keeping your standards high are signs the blue ray is flowing through you. You will not be able to master the blue ray in one day. This will take at least a week, if not longer.

This initiation ritual involves two separate parts. First, you must prepare yourself to be able to tune in to the blue ray. Take out a blue journal, diffuse a blue ray essential oil, or burn some dried flowers from a blue bush or tree while you make your list of songs with the word *blue* in the title. Include at least twenty songs in your list. Then, in your journal, divide a page in half. List ten songs that are happy/positive in one column, and ten songs that are sad/woeful on the other.

Please find some quiet time, meditate for a few minutes, and then listen to a song from each column—one set per day. Jot down your feelings and reactions to each song and its lyrics, if it has them. Answer these questions. How did the song make you feel? What emotions did it generate? What qualities of the blue ray did it portray? Did it convey the darker side of the blue ray, such as sadness? Did any of this music leave a lasting mark on you? Write out any other comments that come to mind. If you want to listen to two sets in a day, make sure you put at least five hours between sessions, so you don't become overwhelmed.

When you have listened to all the songs on your list, write a response to your overall experience listening to the music of the blue ray.

SEA WITCH PURIFICATION RITUAL

The second part of the blue ray initiation is similar to a Hi'uwai, a powerful ritual in native Hawaiian culture that serves to cleanse and purify you from anything that may be blocking you or holding you back. I learned about this ritual while studying Huna Healing with Huna Shaman Serge Kahili King. It's an amazing way to get past obstacles, which is an essential part of being able to tap into the blue ray—so follow these directions to take the first steps.

First, find a body of water that is safe for you to walk into: a lake, a pond, a river, the ocean, or whatever is nearby to where you live. Take a sacred plant with you. Use a plant you love or one that is native to your locale: basil or holy basil, shamrock, or sage will all work quite well, or whatever is accessible and meaningful to you.

As you enter the water, take several leaves with you, and tear the leaves into pieces as you say:

My dearest Archangel Michael, my most sacred guides, masters, gods and goddesses of the blue ray, and in the sacred spirit of water, I welcome you to my

ritual of release. (Tear off a piece of a leaf.) This is for the past and anything that is holding me back from being my highest self. (Throw the piece in the water and tear off another piece.) *This is for surrender to my highest good and perfect path.* (Throw the piece in the water and tear off another piece.) *This represents trust in myself and my personal journey.* (Throw the piece in the water and tear off another piece.) *This is for my creativity and the spirit that thrives within me.* (Throw the piece in the water and tear off another piece.) *This is to acknowledge the gift of permission to be fully who I am now and forever.* (Throw the piece in the water and tear off another piece.) *This is for always trusting my inner guidance no matter what the outside forces say.* (Throw the piece in the water and tear off another piece.) *This is for my gift of speech and communication and for having the courage to always speak my truth and live the truth of who I am.* (Throw the piece in the water and tear off another piece.) *This is in gratitude for the divine protection I am surrounded by all the time.* (Throw the piece in the water and tear off another piece.) *This is for unity with all my fellow human and animal beings.* (Throw the piece in the water and tear off another piece.) *And this is for harmony and peace that everyone and anyone who dwells between the blue sky and the blue sea find comfort in my words, in the power of the blue ray, and enjoy the peace and tranquility of this holy blue ray.* (Throw the last piece(s) in the water and move back to the shore.) *Blessed Be.*

You can repeat this purification ritual anytime you want, even if you are not in proximity to water. You will need to find some sea salt and carry it with you. When you are in need of blue ray renewal, take a pinch of sea salt and place it under your tongue. Say the above words and you will summon Archangel Michael and the blue ray for this purifying and cleansing ceremony.

Please don't rush the blue ray process. It should take you one or two weeks to complete before you move on to the next ray, the indigo ray. If you rush it, you'll defeat the process and halt your ascension through the colored rays of the rainbow.

You may even want to repeat the blue ray processes over the years. They are designed for purification and renewal anytime you feel the need. Do the work and experience the shift for the good.

Chapter 6

THE INDIGO RAY

SEPTEMBER 20–NOVEMBER 9.
THE DAY OF THE WEEK IS SATURDAY.

INDIGO IS A DARK COLOR THAT, LIKE THE BLUE RAY, WAS REVERED BY ancient civilizations, which ascribed to it spiritual associations. By extension due to its connection to the sixth chakra, called *Ajna*, it is linked to the pineal gland, which has been said to be the seat of mystical properties like intuition. The pineal gland is a remarkable organ, connected to our circadian rhythms, which regulate when we sleep and wake. Some wisdom traditions believe that the pineal gland is the connection between our physical world and the world of our minds and spirits.

In ancient Egypt, the Eye of Horus reflected the location of the pineal gland in the human brain. The Hindu Lord Shiva is famous for having three eyes. His right eye represents the sun, his left eye the moon. In the middle of his forehead there is a third eye, and it represents fire. According to the myth, Lord Shiva opened his third eye, saw his lust and greed, and immediately purified it with that fire. In the book *Kundalini Tantra*, Swami Satyananda Saraswati writes that the third eye is also the *eye of intuition*, because it is the doorway through which an individual enters the astral and psychic dimension of consciousness. Edgar Cayce readings suggest that he believed the pineal gland to be the center of our spiritual life wherein the invisible pattern or seed is implanted.

Just imagine that your pineal gland, something as small as a pea, can connect you to cosmic layers of consciousness and awareness. This tiny organ is in tune with the planets, the Pleiades, and even the afterlife. It deserves our attention, our respect, and possibly even our reverence.

By calling in the energy of the indigo ray, we can learn to see through the veil of waking consciousness and into the next level of spirit life. Our human eyes may view the world as it is, but our third eye sees into the cosmic universe and is the home to our sixth sense. You can use the indigo ray's connection to the divine, intuition, and responsibility to self to explore your soul, to go deep within, and to find new ways of directly connecting to deific energy. Use it to replace feelings of unworthiness by embracing your divine birthright to give love, be loved, and share in all of the fruits of this life and life beyond the veil. The veil itself is indigo, but the light behind it is white.

ON YOUR ALTAR

Add the following items and represent the concepts below on your altar to channel the energy of the indigo ray. Remember you are in the high realms now, the place where secrets and celestial truths dwell. Take special care to elevate your altar and honor this ray.

INDIGO RAY ANGEL

The archangel for the indigo ray is Zadkiel. He is the archangel of freedom, forgiveness, and mercy. Zadkiel is frequently pictured with a dagger for having stepped in and saved Abraham from sacrificing Isaac through divine will. We all want mercy, and we love our freedom, but often forgiveness is the toughest challenge in our life experience. Zadkiel is a powerful archangel because he is the one we call on when we have self-doubt or are suffering when we refuse to surrender to what life has brought us.

If we are feeling guilty about our past behavior or choices, then Zadkiel is the archangel to summon for help with self-forgiveness and resistance to reality. Zadkiel communicates that there are no mistakes in life, only the choices we make and the experiences we have based on the choices we have made. If you are filled with self-criticism, that feeling can cloud the mind with the negative impact of a harmful self-image. Archangel Zadkiel helps us to learn from those past mistakes and move forward.

Through Archangel Zadkiel, we can connect to the One Great Spirit and develop a relationship between our self and a higher power. That connection is the superpower of all magic.

Archangel Zadkiel shares his vast knowledge with those who require mercy if they are struggling with past hurts and wounds that have not healed. Through mercy and release, also known as surrender, this grace allows us to accept what is and move forward in life with a lighter heart and a mended soul.

INDIGO RAY ARCHETYPE

The archetype for the color indigo is the Caregiver. It symbolizes caring for your neighbor, generosity to others, compassion, altruism, going out of your way to help others, and being a supporter and advocate, or even a parent. The Caregiver not only cares about others but also does something about that feeling. But watch out that you don't overdo it—being a Caregiver can lead to martyrdom and is easily exploited.

INDIGO RAY ASTROLOGY

The planets associated with the indigo ray are Jupiter and Saturn. Jupiter brings us self-improvement and learning as well as expansion and happiness. Jupiter helps us move forward toward success.

Saturn is the planet of discipline, maturity, responsibility, and stewardship. It brings to light recurring patterns that are holding us back and shows us how we can be the best version of ourselves.

INDIGO RAY FLOWER ESSENCES

The best Bach Flower Remedy for assisting the third eye is hornbeam, which promotes inner vitality and excitement about life. Rock water can also be useful, as it amplifies a sense of inner freedom and emotional liberation. Star of Bethlehem prompts spiritual awakening and internal aliveness, and walnut can be good for protecting new beginnings and fresh starts.

INDIGO RAY CRYSTALS

The crystals that fall under the indigo ray are indigo kyanite, indigo fluorite, dark indigo sodalite, labradorite, lapis lazulite, tanzanite, sodalite, blue obsidian, azurite, amethyst, charoite, iolite, lepidolite, and sugilite. I like choosing the indigo stones that have sparkles in them to pay tribute to the stars in this nighttime cosmic vault.

INDIGO RAY SYMBOLS

As we've discussed, the indigo ray is intimately connected to the concept of the third eye. The third eye is represented by a number of symbols throughout different cultures and wisdom traditions. The Eye of Horus is a powerful symbol to include on your altar as you work with the indigo ray. The icon of Ajna itself is also useful. You may also wish to include a statue of Lord Shiva, or simply any icon representing an eye, such as the Illuminati symbol of an eye within a pyramid. The Greek mati, or evil eye, can also prove to be a powerful representation of all that you are trying to achieve by connecting with the indigo ray (see an overview of this symbol in the blue ray chapter on page 98).

INDIGO RAY ESSENTIAL OILS

Essential oils to facilitate the opening of the third eye and support the indigo ray are lavender, sandalwood, frankincense, clary sage, and bergamot. These are essential oils that can help you transport your consciousness to the next realm.

INDIGO RAY HERBS

Herbal support for the pineal gland assists with preventing calcification or blockage in the pineal gland which inhibits the flow of melatonin. Mucuna, reishi, algae, passionflower, milk thistle, albizzia, gingko, blue lotus, gotu kola, noni, shizandra, moringa, chaga, aloe, and turmeric work nicely to help prevent the calcium buildup.

INDIGO RAY DIVINE ENERGY

As discussed, the most powerful manifestation of indigo ray energy can be found in several Hindu deities. Traditionally, figures of the divine were represented in deep blue, due to their connection between the physical and spiritual worlds. This illustrates the concept of *Brahman*, a concept encapsulating ultimate reality or source. In particular, Shiva and Shakti are wonderful indigo ray divine energies to channel as you work with this ray. These two deities, united in one form, represent male and female energies connecting to form the One Great Spirit of nature and creation.

INDIGO RAY FENG SHUI

In Feng Shui, indigo reflects the color of water and the nighttime sky, which symbolizes both our connection to the cosmos and our journey to greater depths. Indigo is the color associated with the third eye chakra, the pineal gland, and intuition, which is connected to the element of water. When the third eye is open, we feel the cool and calm of the deep blue color, and our vision is clear so our spiritual vision can penetrate the abyss to reveal the truth to us of who we are and what we are meant to be.

WORKING WITH THE INDIGO RAY

Use the practices below to work with the power of the indigo ray. You are working with the powers of heaven here, so you are working in a powerful realm. Tread softly as you enter this level. This is the night garden of the powers of creation.

INDIGO RAY CHAKRA

The chakra of this indigo ray, as we've discussed, is the third eye, *Ajna*. It is the sixth chakra in the line of seven. We come from a spiritual place when we are born, and we return to that same place when we die. From the ages of six through eight we begin to lose our pure connection to spirit because our maturing hormones root us in human sexuality as we evolve. Our focus as we mature through puberty is on ourselves, our bodies, and the physical changes we are experiencing. Hence, spirituality takes second place to the physical changes. Some adults never return to their early childhood connection to sense of the spiritual. Other adults have a longing for that spiritual home with the other side and seek to reawaken the connection we had as children using the third eye and sixth chakra to access the spirit world.

This sixth chakra is filled with wisdom, knowledge, intuition, imagination, and higher consciousness and provides you with a higher purpose and the larger picture of your life and the meaning of life on earth and beyond. Gratitude figures into this chakra as the key force behind being able to open the third eye to see into the worlds beyond this one. But it is not gratitude *for* things or people; it is pure gratitude, minus qualification.

To open this third eye and achieve its blessings, you must begin a practice of meditation and chanting to open the pineal gland, create a vibration, and allow the door to open for you. AUM or OM are the sounds of this chakra and are directly connected to the vibration of the universe. Prayer beads, also called mala beads or japa mala beads, can help you count your audial repetitions. Historically, in the eighth century BCE, seers and mystics in India began to use these strings of beads to count their prayers. *Japa* means "meditation" and *Mala* means "garland."

It is suggested that 108 chants done slowly will unite you with the One Great Spirit and universal creation. Fifty-four of the beads represent the masculine aspects and the other fifty-four represent the feminine, giving you a perfect harmonic balance while you are opening the pineal gland for seeing the invisible other. (More information coming about this practice in the Initiation section on page 141.)

PRANIC BREATHING

+ Gently place your tongue on the roof of your mouth. (To stimulate energy throughout your body.)

+ Gently inhale through your nose for six counts.

- Gently, hold your breath for three counts.

- Carefully exhale through your nose for another six counts.

- Hold your breath for three counts.

This 6-3-6-3 breathing completes one cycle. Please repeat for at least one minute to experience heightened energy and entry into a relaxed and meditative state.

INDIGO RAY DIVINATION

The tarot cards for this indigo ray are The Devil and The World.

INDIGO RAY MAGICAL BIRD

Falcons represent vision and focus, the very qualities of the indigo ray. Indigo and falcons serve the unseen realm because they have the bravery, strength, fluidity, and determination to venture into the unknown. Just as the pineal gland serves our quest beyond our known world, the falcon's qualities help us on our adventure. Falcons are among the fastest-maturing birds, and so have to learn how to take care of themselves and fly at an early age. Their vision is eight times more powerful than humans, which gives them the advantage of seeing deeper and farther than the human eye. They nest high up in the tallest trees and have been clocked at speeds of 200 mph. The falcon selects its prey carefully and dives like a rocket to collect it. The falcon represents patience because she is willing to wait for the right morsel to appear before seizing it. The bravery of the falcon assists our curiosity to know more and see into a different dimension more clearly.

In ancient Egypt, Horus, the son of Isis and Osiris, had the head of a falcon, with the right eye representing the sun and the left eye representing the moon. The falcon was revered and worshipped as the King of the Sky. It was believed he carried messages from the gods to earth and had great authority over earth.

FALCON CEREMONY

You will need a falcon feather and a falcon icon, statue, figurine, or drawing for this ceremony. You can procure a feather from a real falcon (whether found in the wild or purchased online), or you can paint the feather of any bird to match the exquisite brown colorations of the falcon. You will also need a divination tool such as runes, a deck of tarot cards, a pendulum, or any other physical object that will enable you to divine the messages you receive from the great falcon.

Hold the falcon feather in your dominant hand and gently tap it three times on the icon of the falcon.

I tap once for vision, once for focus and once for patience. A gracious greeting to the spirit of the great falcon, Sky King and visionary. Welcome to the ceremony and we call upon your goodness to imbue us with your virtues and wisdom.

We ask you for your gift of crystal

vision that we may see the clearest path and make the right decision.

We ask for your gift of focus that we may see the issue in full clarity and that all things that are not pertinent simply fall away.

We ask for your gift of patience that we may take the time to study all aspects before making a final decision.

We ask for your gift of high perspective that we may see all the parts before coming to a final decision. May your bird's eye view inform us with wisdom and knowledge.

We ask that all possibilities spread before us, and your gifts bring us into the highest realm and brightest light for us to see the way clearly.

At this point, ask your questions, put forth your dilemma, or express your conundrum. Use your divination tool, whether a pendulum, runes, a tarot card, or anything else that resonates with you to obtain answers to questions. When you are finished, say the following words:

In deepest gratitude for your willingness to share your gifts, we have obtained the answer we seek. Thank you for joining us and for your generosity. We release you back into your sky kingdom with love, appreciation, and our gratitude for all that you are. Blessed Be.

Whatever you were concerned about should be answered by this ceremony. If it feels right, you were successful. If it doesn't feel right, meditate on your discomfort. Remember the falcon and do not rush to judgment. Wait at least a week to see if new information comes forth that will make this answer correct. Remember the three virtues of the falcon: vision, focus, and patience. They go hand in hand with indigo ray magic.

INDIGO RAY PLANT MAGIC

When you work with the earth, you may want to plant flowers for the indigo ray. Used for dyes in the past are true indigo, also called French indigo, natal indigo, and Guatemalan indigo. Other indigo color flowers include the deep iris, empire blue butterfly bush, perennial geranium, bellflower, blue false indigo, columbine, lobelia, lupine, sweet pea, birdbill dayflower, mountain larkspur, desert bluebells, and scabiosa. You may find other varieties in your garden store, but always choose the darkest of the blue blossoms.

If you want a dark violet-blue tree, you'll need to plant indigo, jacaranda, or the lovely rose of Sharon. I have always been a huge fan of jacaranda because when they dress up for spring and summer, their explosion of blossoms dazzles even the highest of archangels. It's an excellent tree for meditation and quiet inner contemplation because it exudes grandeur and joy.

INDIGO RAY WITCHCRAFT

The witches falling under the indigo ray are: The Ancestral Witch, who honors their ancestors year-round by connecting with them spiritually and magically. The Animist Witch, who sees the universe as a living entity with no difference between animals, people, or material objects. The Augury Witch, who divines omens, signs, and symbols. The Ceremonial Witch, who is dedicated to ceremonies and rituals calling on specific beings for their magic. The Divination Witch, who uses many occult methods to predict the future or to receive information about the present circumstances. The Shamanic Witch, who uses the powers of the other side along with the magic and medicine of plants and animals. And finally, the Solitary Witch, a witch of any type who prefers to practice alone without a coven.

Ceremony is important to the Ceremonial Witch. Here are some ceremonies that you might enjoy using.

RITUALS FOR THE CEREMONIAL WITCH

The Pagan and Celtic calendar of the year follows the movement of the season, and Rainbow Witches tune into these rhythms and follow nature as she turns her head and dances through the seasons. Here are a few derived from the practices of the Ceremonial Witch that you may wish to add to your practice, particularly as you investigate the indigo ray.

BURNING BOWL RITUAL TO UNBURDEN THE PAST YEAR AND CREATE ANEW

You will need:

- A fireproof bowl suitable for burning
- Matches or a lighter
- Felt pen
- Paper (or flash paper, which you can purchase at a magic store; this will amplify your statements)
- A wand
- White stone

Wheel of the Year

First, meditate or perform any other practice that helps you find inner peace. Never do this ceremony if you are angry, upset, or feel unbalanced.

Second, write down what you wish to leave behind in the past year. Do not assign blame. Simply state the facts.

Third, take responsibility. If you had any part in creating the things you wish to burn and erase, write down how you may have participated in thought or deed.

Fourth, crumple the papers and place them in the bowl, then ignite them with the lighter. Say the following words:

> Witch's power, in this hour
>
> Invoke the winds of change.
>
> May they blow gently now
>
> As I release the pain,
>
> Never praised, never lost,
>
> Thus, only good remains.
>
> Blessed Be.

Fifth, extinguish the fire and go into a short meditation. Find one word that represents what you desire for the coming year. When you know that one word, come out of your meditation and write the word on your stone in felt pen. Keep this stone for a year on your altar to remind you of your focus.

BLESSING A HOUSE USING ESSENTIAL OILS

To protect a house and its inhabitants from misfortune, you can perform this ritual every year, or just when a person moves in.

Moving into a new home is always a special occasion and, with friends and loved ones gathered around, a great opportunity to bless both the house and its new occupants. It is also a good time to "clean house" of any past energies that no longer belong there and to make room for the new family and its happy future. Open with this statement:

What a happy day this is! [Names of new homeowners] *are moving into their new home and we are here to celebrate and bless this wonderful new beginning.*

This is an exciting time, the start of a new adventure, the foundation of the next chapter in their lives together. Their lives will be lived out under this roof. Decisions will be made at this table that affect their future. A family will learn and grow within these walls, and we all wish our friends years of peace, safety, and happiness here. Many celebrations will be held in this house, many milestones will be marked; we expect that there will be many opportunities to celebrate joy here. But before we go on with today's celebration, we take a few minutes to acknowledge and bless the role this house will play in our friends' lives in the coming years.

Take a small vial of diluted essential oils and walk from room to room placing a small drop of oil in a corner of each room in the house while saying a word or two of blessings appropriate for each room. For example, say the following words while anointing:

IN THE KITCHEN: *May the food prepared in this room always nourish those who eat here. May it build strong bodies and inspire wise and peaceful minds, and may there always be plenty in this house. This essential oil blend contains Melissa (lemon balm), called the "elixir of life" by ancient Greeks.*

This oil will ensure that food served in this room builds strength and revive the energies of those who live here.

IN THE BEDROOM: *May love abide here. May the day end gently here. May the nights be peaceful and may sleep come easily. And may every morning be welcomed with a smile of gratitude for another day of love and joy and prosperity for this family.* This essential oil blend contains tea tree essential oil for harmony; rose for love, peace and beauty; and sandalwood essential oil, which not only enhances your times of prayer and meditation but, as an aphrodisiac, makes love even more exciting in this space.

IN THE FAMILY ROOM: *Life happens here.* This family room is dedicated to the growth of this family in every area of their lives. The essential oils we place here are vetiver essential oil for protection, sage to cleanse, and myrrh to lift and enlighten their journey.

May they grow strong and wise, both individually and together, in this space. May they learn respect and appreciation for one another in this place. May they come to a greater understanding of the unique gifts of each of the members of this family, and may they grow in love within these walls. May that love reach beyond these walls to touch and bless the lives of others.

When you have processed through the entire house saying a special sentence of blessing in each room, return to the room in which you started. To conclude, add this closing statement:

> This is a new beginning. With the essential oil of clary sage, we cleanse the ethers of any past negativity. With bergamot and rose essential oils, we infuse this space with joy, love, peace, and beauty. Today we cleanse this house of any remnants of the past, that it may be free to provide only blessings for this family.

An additional option is to put essential oils in a diffuser and place it in the room in which you conclude, saying:

We leave a diffuser with essential oils in this room so that the air in this house will remain alive with these blessings and intentions. (Note: Be sure to follow cautions for diffusing around children and pets.)

Conclude by saying: *With these sacred essential oils, we put into motion energies that vitalize and renew each day. May times of joy be multiplied many times over. May opportunities abound within these walls, and may the occasional moments of sadness, sorrow, or concern be washed away by the tears of love and the soothing sound of laughter.* (You may also wish to add a prayer to the ending if that is appropriate for your gathering.)

CEREMONY FOR IMBOLC, THE END OF WINTER, AND THE COMING OF SPRING

When this feast day occurs, you will want to honor it and use your powers to exit the winter and welcome the spring. The goddess Brighid is the center of this feast.

You will need seven candles, and one each for as many participants as you wish. Seven candles sit on the main altar and everyone else holds their own candle for this ceremony. You will also need a bundle of flexible rushes, reeds, lavender stalks, paper slim cuttings, straw, or pipe cleaners.

The leader of the ritual should say the following words:

Let us gather for a moment in silence to prepare ourselves for the exit of winter and the welcoming of new growth. Say, as you move from dark to light:

> May wintry gods take timely flight
>
> And wait until next darkened night
>
> To cover us with ice and snow
>
> Begone you now, arise and go.
>
> Allow the spring to birth anew
>
> The calf and lamb be born in dew
>
> Let all rejoice set bells to ring
>
> We welcome in our Lady Spring.

Play the song "Ode to Brigid." You'll find many options for the audio on YouTube.

As you play the song, light the center candle on the alter. Say, *For Brighid.* From that candle, light everyone's candle. Form a circle.

> For the first light of Spring, we light this candle.
>
> For the new beginning, we light this candle.
>
> For the seeds we plant, we light this candle.
>
> For strong growth and healthy crops, we light this candle.
>
> For the ample harvest, we light this candle.
>
> For gratitude for our families and lives, we light this candle.
>
> For the joy we create this year, we light this candle.

Blessed Be. Everyone repeats, *Blessed Be.*

It is customary for everyone to make the Saint Brigid's Cross from the reeds and straw you have gathered, and then enjoy some tea and cakes. Set up a table with supplies. (There are several lovely videos on YouTube showing how to set an Imbolc table, which I recommend.) Enjoy some tea and lemon tarts to welcome in the spring.

INITIATION INTO THE INDIGO RAY

When you reach the indigo ray, it means you are serious about learning and practicing magic and you are willing to begin with yourself as a canvas.

The first step in working the indigo ray is to establish a spiritual practice that you do daily. Repetition is powerful, and a good way to initiate yourself into routine.

We introduced the concept of prayer beads, or mala beads, in our discussion of indigo ray chakra work. These beads are so powerful, particularly when combined with a chant of some sort that pleases you. If you don't have mala beads or they don't speak to you, there are alternatives from many different cultures. For example, in the Christian religion it is alleged that the Desert Fathers carried a pouch of stones with them to count their prayers in the third century. It wasn't until 1350 that the actual rosary was strung, which consisted of 150 beads to match the recitation of the 150 Psalms as a spiritual practice. You can also derive your own system for counting prayers, chants, or meditations for opening yourself to indigo ray energy.

However, if you are ambivalent, I would recommend acquiring a string of mala beads and chanting by using AUM or OM. These two words are sacred sounds in Hinduism and have been used for millennia to focus awareness and invoke the divine. If you are unfamiliar with pronunciation, the Internet has plenty of YouTube videos demonstrating how to verbalize these sounds correctly, and how to chant with them. You could also chant *om mani padme hum* in sync with a musical arrangement (again, YouTube has a wealth of content for you to peruse). You can also find your own words, or your own mantras, to chant. These are only suggestions for you. Chanting is an important practice to explore when you begin to initiate yourself into the indigo ray, because it triggers the tetrahedron bone in your nose to resonate, which results in stimulation of the pineal gland.

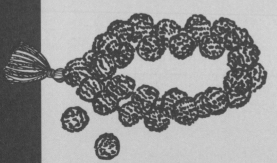

Some examples of other styles of chanting are Ambrosian, Beneventan, Gallican, Mozarabic, Old Roman, Hebrew, Ravenna, West African, Peruvian, and a host of other chants from many nationalities, belief systems, and cultures. Find your chant style of choice, or simply make up your own: the point is to clear your mind, open your third eye, and prepare yourself for the indigo ray over time.

Start out with ten to fifteen minutes a day and work your way up to thirty minutes of chanting. Journal your experiences in your indigo journal and use your pen with deep purple or indigo ink. Describe how you felt before and after your session, and continue writing about your feelings for at least a week. Then review what you wrote and journal what you learned. Once you have a practice in place, allow the practice to take you deeper and deeper into your soul. Capture your journey and experiences in your journal.

When your practice is part of your daily routine, it's time to reach out to Archangel Zadkiel. Below is a meditation you can use to meet him. Use this to explore your inner wisdom and to gain more spiritual knowledge, forgive the past and open new portals to experiences the emotions of joy and living with grace.

ARCHANGEL ZADKIEL MEDITATION

Find a quiet place where you can be alone and unobserved. Start with your breath. Use a gentle inhale and exhale and follow the breath as it travels into and out of your body. Notice the temperature of your breath. Is it warm or cool? Is it shallow or full? Whatever you discover, allow it to be in this moment and surrender into it.

Repeat the words *I surrender, I surrender, I surrender* three times. Then say, *Here and now is perfect. I am in the prefect place. I am breathing the perfect breath. I am thinking perfect thoughts. I am me. It is all perfect. Blessed Be.*

Continue breathing and allow your senses to expand to include any presence that may wish to join you. When you feel it, say, *Welcome Zadkiel. It is my joy and honor to meet you. Thank you for coming to me.*

Wait for a response. You should feel Zadkiel in your heart (the fourth chakra) and solar plexus (the third chakra). When you do, say, *I am asking that you open my heart, release my loving nature, and allow forgiveness to flow. I am your student and I wish to serve with more grace and compassion.* This is the time to add any personal requests for specific healings. When you are finished, take three deep, full breaths, fill your lungs completely, and hold for three seconds. Release the breath slowly, and with it, the old emotions, and let them dissipate into the atmosphere. Take two more breaths the same way and intake the light of Zadkiel. You may feel a mist around you. That's not unusual. When you have completed your three breaths (the number of divinity), say, *Thank you Archangel Zadkiel for showing me release, surrender, forgiveness, and healing. Thank you for the peace I feel and the joy I have within.* Take one more breath and exhale with a sound of release—*Ahhhhhh*—and feel the power of Zadkiel's wings lift you higher and higher. You might add, *Please come again. I love you.* Allow Zadkiel to depart. You may physically feel a cool breeze as he leaves. Open your eyes when you are ready.

Close your session with a prayer of gratitude, *Blessed Be all the angels and archangels, and especially Zadkiel who visited me today. I am grateful for the gifts, the enlightenment, and the peace that has been given to me. Blessed Be.*

Don't rush this journey. When you are fully back in your body, journal what you felt and learned. You can always return to this ray and this exercise anytime you feel the need for a refreshment of his gifts.

Congratulations: your daily practice of meditation and your strong connection with the Archangel Zadkiel have initiated you into the energy of the indigo ray. You have opened your third eye and begun to experience what that feels like. In the years to come, if you keep up the practice, your third eye will open even more, increasing your feelings of peace, joy, and clarity, as well as the ability to see the big picture for yourself and in the lives of others.

Come back to this ray frequently. Restore your practice if you fall off your routine, and definitely count on Archangel Zadkiel to keep your heart open and your compassion flowing. You are at the doorway of telepathy, clairvoyance, and many other gifts of precognition, having the foreknowledge of an event coming up, lucid dreaming, when you know you are dreaming but the event feels real, and astral travel, which is the ability of a person's spirit to travel to distant places and return. It all begins right here with the indigo ray.

Chapter 7

THE VIOLET RAY

November 10–December 31.
The day of the week is Sunday.

THE COLOR VIOLET IS A COMBO-COLOR MADE UP OF THE CALMING qualities of blue and the enthusiastic fire of red. This blend makes it a dynamic color full of passion and bubbling over with expression of that emotion. It also combines the balance of blue and the sensitivity of that color. Deep violet is associated with royalty, luxury, power, and ambition. It was the color worn by kings and queens, emperors like Julius Caesar, Zeus, and high-ranking clergy. In Egyptian times, purple dyes, especially the highly valued Tyrian purple made from small mollusks called murex snails, were reserved for the rulers, who were believed to be divine. The vibrational qualities of the color violet bring independence, inspiration, vision, and the ability to see the whole picture and creatively figure out how to make things better.

Violet encompasses artistic and unique qualities such as high intuition, leadership ranking, and spirituality. On the other side of royalty and privilege, there is a dedicated sense of humanitarianism that violet embodies as well as its visionary and artistic proclivities. Because violet lifts the mind and soul, it conveys an otherworldly feeling, as if mere mortals are unworthy of its glory. In the late eighteenth century there was a craze called *violettomania*. It described the use of the color by Claude Monet and by Camille Pissarro, who insisted trees were purple. However, the violet ray can also mean immaturity in the sense that one clings to an unrealistic ideal when it is clear that it is unfeasible. At one time in the evolution of humanity, the color purple was only available to the wealthy and the powerful, hence it can appear a bit entitled and arrogant.

In her writings, Alice Bailey defined the violet ray as an experience of the higher vibrations of your soul that assist you in living in a place of loving power as opposed to a place of fear and powerlessness. This is the color of intuition and psychic connection. It is a sensitive color and must be creative in order to survive. The color encourages compassion and love for others as well as a calm and strong connection to the spiritual realm. It is a highly vibrational color with high expectations because it is one step away from the universal connection and unity with the One Great Spirit; therefore it requires one to step up and be fully present and active. It is time for the violet ray to take center stage as we become full-fledged Rainbow Witches.

ON YOUR ALTAR

Use the following items and concepts to channel indigo ray energy on your altar.

VIOLET RAY ANGEL

The Archangel Gabriel is our guide, wise master, and guardian for this ray. Archangel Gabriel is an angel who warns humanity of impending disasters and also portends events of joy. He was the one who told Mary she was with child, who was the Spirit of God. Gabriel awakened Joseph and told him to escape to Nazareth in the middle of the night. Archangel Gabriel is known to be the herald of visions, one of the highest-ranking angels next to Michael and Raphael, and he is a first-class messenger.

Because his assignment is to guard, protect, and warn humanity, he also generates self-expression, is a protector of the arts, and fosters communication in all forms, whether through mass media or on social media, as well as from the next world: Gabriel is present in any type of clairvoyant readings, channeling, automatic writing, and psychic endeavors. He rules over mental clarity, as well as related spiritual gifts like clairvoyance, clairaudience, clairsentience, clairgustance, and any other ability that could be considered a clair.

Archangel Gabriel will assist you in manifesting all of your divinely guided inspirations and creative thoughts. He will help you make them real. This is his charter. You will feel his presence when you sense a sudden urge to take action, or when you have the spark of a thought that you feel is divinely guided. Archangel Gabriel is probably the most accessible of all the archangels because he is around us all the time. He is the human-divine connection that keeps the channel open and flowing between heaven and earth. He oversees all creative and spiritual works.

If you have a day of doubt, call upon him for guidance. He's right there, so no need for any dramatic ceremonials: just ask him in a whisper. He'll bring you unimagined clarity and insight. With Gabriel in your orbit, you have a partner to help with your success in any lane you choose.

His color is white, but that color is considered to be an outcast on the color spectrum, so the next in line for colors is violet. We'll give him white light for purity and the violet ray for psychic activities and inter-realm conveyances.

VIOLET RAY ASTROLOGY

The planet for this color is the moon. Some have said it's Saturn or Venus, but it's actually the moon, because the moon is the governor of our instincts and our unconscious minds. The unconscious controls our lives until we investigate it and train it to work for our greatest good. The moon, like the violet ray, connects us with cosmic energies and the all-present power that encompasses every one of us and dwells within us.

VIOLET RAY ARCHETYPE

The archetype for this ray is the Sage. This person has gone through the challenges of materialism and the ego and given up all attachment to them in favor of connection to the divine and helping humanity through psychic connections with the One Great Spirit. The Sage has learned through a lifetime of experiences that one cannot live in this world alone and all their accomplishments are the result of the team behind them. The Sage understands weighing and praying: weighing all avenues of action and praying for the guidance to make the correct choice. The Sage does not get thrown off course because of high winds, change, or circumstances. Rather, the Sage weighs the possibilities, gauges the oppressor, and marches right through conflict, holding their banner high. Once the Sage steps into action, victory is imminent.

VIOLET RAY FLOWER ESSENCES

The flower essences for this ray are cherry plum, which promotes emotional composure, calm and balance; gentian for optimism and confidence; willow for happy and joyous participation.

VIOLET RAY CRYSTALS

Amethyst leads the pack along with charoite, sugilite, purple lepidolite, purpurite, ametrine, alexandrite, purple jasper, chalcedony, and purple fluorite. Many stores sell dyed or color-treated purple stones, so beware of the hype and fakery.

VIOLET RAY SYMBOLS

If the color violet ray were to be a symbol, it would be represented as a crown for royalty, a sash for nobility, an amethyst for psychic powers, selenite for the moon, a symbol for magic like a triskele or a Celtic knot, a crystal ball, or an icon of the moon.

VIOLET RAY ESSENTIAL OILS

The essential oils represented by the violet ray are lavender, lavandin, and spike lavender. These are heavenly essences and possess the properties to keep us safe, pure, and able to reach higher realms.

VIOLET RAY DIVINE ENERGY

The deities associated with the color purple are Zeus, Hades, Hecate, and Hathor. Zeus, of course, as ultimate ruler, Hades because of the dark color of the purple sky and wealth, Hecate because of her purple mantle, and Hathor because she is Mistress of the Midnight Sky.

VIOLET RAY FENG SHUI

In Feng Shui, the color violet represents wealth. More than anything, it is a symbol of what is of value to you. For example, in some parts of the world, having a dozen cattle is a sign of wealth. In Western countries, money may be the sign of wealth. In essence, it represents what you value most in your life. Make sure you are clear on what that is, then wear it like a royal sash.

WORKING WITH THE VIOLET RAY

The practices below will help you work with the power of the violet ray. Remember, we are working with the highest energies of the rainbow and of the cosmos. Pay attention and stay in the place of universal power and knowingness. If you are not feeling in your power, then wait a few days until you are. Balance the seventh chakra and test the waters. When you feel strong, congruent, and ready to launch even deeper, then you will be ready to work with the violet ray.

VIOLET RAY CHAKRA

The seventh chakra is *Sahasrara*, meaning "infinite," the chakra that activates divine energy. When this chakra is balanced and open, the connection with the cosmos is as easy as dialing a phone number and saying, "Hello."

A healthy and balanced Sahasrara brings a positive attitude and the ability to always see things as opportunities not difficulties. We are no longer ruled by our egos, but by emotions and qualities like compassion, empathy, gratitude, and acceptance. Negative thinking is automatically erased and in its place joy, bliss, and optimism reign. We become closer to our divine selves and the absorption and understanding of what peace truly means.

If our seventh chakra, Sahasrara, is blocked, we may feel disillusioned and want to give up. Life may feel blah, and we may suffer melancholy and feel bored. We will feel endlessly restless. When this chakra is open, all of life feels magnificent and magical and we are overflowing with joy, excitement, and optimism. No wall is too high to scale; we feel as if we have guidance helping us through the maze. We feel connected to the powers above and happily seek counsel from entities beyond this realm. Open this chakra by connecting to the violet ray and take yourself through the initiation process to come. You will know by your feelings and clarity in your mind if your chakra is open or not.

VIOLET RAY PLANT MAGIC

The flowers for your garden for this ray are lavender, verbena, clematis, bellflower, dwarf iris, balloon flower, catmint, salvia, allium, monkshood, Alpine betony, lily of the Nile, anemone, bee orchid, bittersweet nightshade, wild indigo, bell heather, wild hyacinth, China aster, lilac, and many other varieties of orchid. Notice how these flowers are elegant and beautifully apportioned. They have uplifting fragrances and embody the violet ray in everything they manifest.

Violet and purple trees are the jacaranda, climbing wisteria, royal empress, crepe myrtle, chaste tree, lilac bush, magnolia royal purple, mountain laurel, grapes, and the orchid tree.

VIOLET RAY DIVINATION

The tarot cards are The Wheel of Fortune, The Star, and the Moon.

VIOLET RAY HERBS

Purple herbs are rosemary, lavender, purple basil, Krishna purple, wild oregano, purple sinuate, purple shiso, periwinkle, purple radish, purple hyssop, and purple mustard. There are more international brands of purple herbs, too.

VIOLET RAY MAGICAL BIRD

The ancient Romans believed that their king was protected by a beautiful snow-white bird, who lived in his house. Because it possessed the magical talent of absorbing sickness, it was able to heal the monarch and carry away any illness. For that reason, the Caladrius represents expulsion, exorcism, and the healing that results from removing toxic influences and things that are blocking or harming you.

The Caladrius can take on another's misfortune or ill health and remove it because it knows its own power and strength. It is able to transform that pain into something good and return again, having done its work. It represents strength that is anything but codependent, and is an independent source of self-knowledge and inner resolve.

When we need to remove something or someone that is troubling us, we invite in the magic of Caladrius to transform our situation. This being's magic simply replaces one energy for another. What may once have been negative or consuming can be changed to positive and nourishing.

CALADRIUS BANISHMENT RITUAL

To work with Caladrius magic, make sure you have a visual symbol or an icon of what you wish to remove. If you choose a person, have a photo of them with you. You will also need a pure white feather, your wand, a clear quartz crystal, and sparkly dust in the form of eco clear glitter. (I like to use TodayGlitter, which decomposes in air and water because plastic has been replaced with a eucalyptus extract. Two other great brands are BioGlitter, which is made from cellulose, and Eco Glitter Fun, which is a completely biodegradable cellulose film product.)

With your wand, draw a large circle in the air. Then draw an imaginary branch. On the branch hold the white feather. Say the following words:

> Hail, Caladrius, come away from your palace and teach us your healing magic. We await your arrival and welcome you with open arms. Your branch is ready for you.

You may feel a slight breeze. You may sense a new presence. When you do, proceed. Focus on the circle where Caladrius has landed.

> Our mission here today is a sacred task that you, Caladrius, can manage with ease.

Clearly state the illness, problem, condition, or thought that requires removal.

We ask that you take away _____ and remove it forever. Transform the condition into something beneficial and return it here. May it be a swift journey and a safe return trip while we await your return. Hold the crystal in your hand.

> Now is the time we release _____ and we thank it for the lessons it has taught us and the moment it brought us to

right here and right now. We release it in love because it has served us, and we accept only good and only new, fresh energy in its place.

Use your wand to banish the negative energy and use the feather to fan it away and say, *Begone now and forever.*

Use your feather to create a circle of fresh energy around the person or thing (symbolized) and say, *Gratefully, we accept this new energy as a replacement for that which we no longer need. May this bright, white light fill us with joy, elation as we claim full healing in this moment and forever after. Caladrius has brought us the miracle and we accept the magic in this moment.* Deploy the glitter and use it generously.

With gratitude we release Caladrius from his sacred duty and send him back to the castle that protects and nourishes his beautiful spirit. Blessed Be.

Ask others to repeat *Blessed Be* after you three times. Erase the circle you drew with your feather. Bow in deep gratitude to the place Caladrius landed and close your ceremony.

It is wise after a healing to not discuss the process or talk about it. Let it be. Let it manifest. Put it out of your mind and go on with your day/ evening. Overprocessing a healing is like dissecting a ghost. Let the magic work in its own time frame and leave it alone. We should never interfere with timing. The healing may be instantaneous, or it may take some time. Remember the falcon and have patience. The healing is done, but how it will manifest is up to universal magic in quantum space and time.

VIOLET RAY WITCHCRAFT

There are other types of witches that connect with this ray: The Angel Witch, who works with angels and angel magic. The Cosmic Witch, who uses the placement of the planets, stars, and moon for their magic. The Crystal Witch, who uses crystals for spells, rituals, and magic. The Hedge Witch, who *jumps the hedge*, meaning moves easily between the earthly and astral planes. The Lunar/Moon Witch, who uses the cycles of the moon as their magical platform. The Right-Handed Witch, who believes in divine unions and works a path reunifying human and divine. And finally, the Swamp Witch, who holds a disdain for social norms and rejects a repressive materialistic society, finding the darker secrets of natural magic in the swamps.

CRYSTAL WITCH MAGIC FOR RAINBOW WITCHES

Crystals, which are made in the earth, are profound carriers of energy. Many of them have strong grounding properties because of their connection to earth energies, while others connect you to the cosmic realms. All of them connect to the rainbow, which makes them intensely powerful tools that are practically indispensable for anyone wishing to work with rainbow witchcraft. There are hundreds, if not thousands, of crystals to choose from, and they all have energetic properties. So, to avoid frustration, you can begin with twelve crystals and gemstones that contain the energies you will need.

Crystals can transmit energy from one source to another, purify the environment from negative energy fields in the air or atmosphere, neutralize the electromagnetic currents that can protect your computer from negative static, protect the environment from harmful interference, and uplift your spirits when you're in a bad mood. They can clear and cleanse, wash away unwanted vibrations just as water washes away dirt, focus your thoughts, dreams, and concerns, increase psychic awareness, activate positive energies, deflect negative energy away from you and your environment, and heal in so many other ways by amplifying your intentions and exuding heart-centered energy and healing to your minds, bodies, and souls.

Crystals have the ability to open the pathways of energy from the brain, tissues, and cells to the entire body as well as channel energy from the places you select; like from nature to your body; from your hand to another's ailment or pain. They can stimulate, as in stir-up energy, awaken dormant impulses, and enliven the chakras. Think of crystals as the Rainbow Witch's best friends and put them to use frequently in your magic.

#1 CLEAR QUARTZ

Color: Clear

Qualities: Power, Energy, Clarity

Assists: New beginnings, fresh energies, enthusiasm for life, dreams, personal freedom, accomplishments, goals, achievements, and success.

Many ancient societies believed quartz crystals to be the direct incarnations of divine cosmic energy. Some believed these crystals were, in fact, gods themselves. Easily programmable, quartz is one of the most receptive crystals for positive affirmations and even stores them for you. Quartz enhances the communication between this plane and the heavenly realm. It is believed that these ancient rocks contain secrets from past civilizations and ancient records, and that they can communicate with each other through that energy pattern. They are the very breath and heart of a dragon according to the ancient Chinese.

#2 AMETHYST

Color: Purple

Qualities: Psychic, Temperance, Protection

Assists: Sobriety, restraint, temperance, overindulgence, increases intelligence, shrewdness in business, connects purpose and action, and stills the restless mind. Enhances serenity and composure. Heals personal losses, aids in grief recovery, builds strength, enhances flexibility, invites in peace and happiness, and raises psychic vibrations.

Many gems are simply quartz crystals colored by the environments to which they are exposed. Amethyst gets its color from iron found at specific points in the crystalline structure. The color ranges from pale violet to deep purple.

The color purple is one of the highest vibrational colors on the spectrum. Amethyst is known as nature's tranquilizer, The Artist's Stone, The Composer's Stone, The Painter's Stone, The Poet's Stone, and The Inventor's Stone because it contains the creative energy of the universe This is the master stone for the work of the healing artist. Amethyst embodies the connection between heaven and earth and the realms of the seen and the unseen. It is the ultimate connector of the realms beyond.

#3 CITRINE

Color: Yellow

Qualities: Success, Abundance, Personal Power. It comes in various shades of yellow.

Assists: Intelligence, inner wisdom, concentration, and mental clarity. Transforms fear and anxiety into productivity and controls the abuse of power and megalomania in a leader. Balances yin-yang energy and stabilizes emotions. Given as a gift to a newborn at birth, a citrine stone will encourage health, happiness, inquisitiveness, confidence, and inner wisdom as the child grows.

Citrine has been called *the stone of the mind*. Ancient cultures believed that placing a citrine on the forehead of an elder would increase his psychic power. It's believed to be able to transmute negative thinking into optimism and alter poverty consciousness into abundance-thinking, resulting in prosperity.

Citrine is used for balancing group energy and creating wise management. A very sunny and cheerful stone, it clears negative energy without absorbing it and clears other stones as well. It makes room for happiness and light to replace negative feelings. The gold color of the stone brings much success, but take care and keep it indoors as it will fade in the sunlight.

#4 ROSE QUARTZ

Color: Pink

Qualities: Love, Balance, Forgiveness

Assists: Heart-centered living, self-love, beautiful dreams. Provides protection against malicious gossip, dissolves worry and fears, and encourages forgiveness of self and others, dissipates grudges, calls in love, attracts romantic partnerships, builds on inner peace and contentment, allows change to occur naturally, and enhances the shift as an instrument of spiritual growth.

Love is the heartbeat of creation and the very conduit that holds our cosmos together. At the center of creation is intelligence. Intelligence is love and love is intelligence. Without the adhesive energy of love, everything we know dissipates and disappears. Hence, rose quartz is the universal healer of all the ages and our world. It emits a lovely vibration of gentleness to remove negativity and usher in the forces of universal love. Egyptians carved face masks of rose quartz for the dead to wear so they would be sure to attract love in the afterlife.

Rose quartz transmutes sorrow into joy and turns negativity into optimism. It encourages us to turn inward, discover the core of self-love, and allow that quality to expand from the inside outward. From this core of love and forgiveness we can easily extend that love to others using rose quartz as the catalyst.

#5 FLUORITE

Color: Multiple

Qualities: Clarity, Purpose, Order

Assists: A flawless ideal of perfect health, the intellect, emotions, and overall well-being. It purifies, cleanses, purges, balances, dissipates viruses, cold, flu, and provides a layer of protection against infection. It clears up mental fog and aids in the use of intuition. It contributes to psychic and spiritual wholeness by bringing mental order and clarity to any spiritual path or awakening.

Fluorite is called The Gemstone of Discernment by many in the gemological and metaphysical worlds. The hues stretch across the color spectrum, and each fluorite possesses a unique healing quality.

Blue is for orderly thoughts. Chinese is for disease protection. Purple is for mystical intuition. Colorless is for purification and energy. Green is for cleansing. Yellow is for creativity. Magenta is for forgiveness and understanding. Rainbow is for flexibility. Pink is for cheer and joy. Black is for astral cleansing.

Fluorite's overall qualities stabilize energies, including those of heaven to earth, the dynamics in groups, personal relationships, and one's inner world. This stabilizing energy brings order out of chaos and aligns the mental, physical, and spiritual realms into equal balance. Fluorite promotes impartiality and grounds cosmic and spiritual energies. It guides one away from anxiety into tranquility by neutralizing negative energy.

#6 BLACK TOURMALINE

Color: Black

Qualities: Grounding, Protection, Stability

Assists: Inspires altruism, protects against negativity, grounds energy, eliminates toxic metals, increases physical vitality, enhances stability, evens out mood swings, creates high spirits in the face of doom and gloom, increases overall well-being, and has the power to repel an evil spell and send it back to the sender like a boomerang. It clears the mind and soothes panic attacks.

Black tourmaline is renowned for its protection and ability to repel negative energy. Also called Schorl, black tourmaline retains an electrical charge when heated, making it able to store the charge once received.

It keeps a balance of linear energy flow, from top to bottom, by way of its external ridges that are believed to connect heaven and earth. That's why it is a great balancer and also protects against electromagnetic radiation (EMR) and evil spells.

#7 JADE

Color: Multiple

Qualities: Abundance, Love Balance

Assists: Dreams and dreamers, brings clear insight, stimulates prosperity, calms a stormy mind, encourages healing, aids healers in their work, brings emotional healing to past hurts, attracts romance, and stabilizes emotions. This is a key stone for healers, physicians, psychologists, and teachers.

Jade, known as The Dreamer's Stone and The Stone from Heaven, has been used in cultures ranging from China to Middle and Central America, to New Zealand (Māori), Australia (Aborigines), the Inuits, and ancient Celtic peoples. It is believed that jade blesses and cleanses all who encounter it.

There are two kinds of Jade. Nephrite is the most common and used for carvings, weapons, talismans, and burials. Nephrite is associated with grace, purity, beauty, and dreams. Jadeite, the rarest and more expensive type of jade, has a slightly different meaning and purpose than nephrite jade. Jadeite deals with health, longevity, and love. Wearing, holding, and meditating with jadeite jade improves health, calmness, and longevity. Jadeite is credited with opening one's heart to love when worn in jewelry.

There are many colors of jade available. Each has a different focus and expertise. Black wards off negative assaults, including self-condemnation and spells. Blue calms the mind and brings peace. Brown grounds and connects to the earth. Green symbolizes health and the heart. Lavender supplies spiritual nourishment to the soul. Orange brings about joy and elation. Yellow is cheerful and energetic, and helps accomplish goals. White aids in decision-making.

#8 TURQUOISE

Color: Blue-green

Qualities: Protection, Energy, Serenity

Assists: Devotion, clear communication, fidelity, spontaneous romance, strength of purpose. Cleanses energy centers, enhances the ability to see all sides of an issue, generates freedom, and integrates all the extenuating parts into a perfect whole. It strengthens friendships and removes obstacles to happiness.

King Tut's death mask in 1324 BCE was emblazoned with turquoise stones presumably as protection and for wholeness in the afterlife. Turquoise helps us honor ourselves as creatures of the divine mind and tools of creation. No better stone helps us see all of our traits—negative and positive—in one light and use them to make a perfect whole. Turquoise beads have been discovered in tombs dating back to Iraq 5000 BCE.

Turquoise is a master stone of unification. It builds strength, reinforces our capabilities, and brings encouragements for our endeavors. It fosters honest communication from the heart. Hailed as a stone of friendship, it brings friends closer together and strengthens the bond of friendship between them.

#9 RED JASPER

Color: Red

Qualities: Strength, Courage, Healing

Assists: Reduces stress, induces tranquility, brings peace and relaxation, and hones inner strength to support courage, cleanses negative energy, soothes nerves. It is the martial artist of the gem world because it brings inner calm to face the fierce enemy in battle. It is an excellent worry stone because it lends emotional support. It balances yin and yang.

Called The Supreme Nurturer, red jasper is a natural healer with the grounding properties of stability and strength and provides protection courage and wisdom to the wearer. It is a dense, opaque microcrystalline variety of quartz. Its name comes from the Greek word *iaspis*, meaning "jasper." It is imbued with qualities of courage and shamanic wisdom and holds deep, grounding earth energy.

There are many varieties of jasper, each being affected by the mineral and chemical content of what was surrounding it at the time of formation. Ocean jasper is uplifting and restorative, picture jasper draws in security and connection, leopard skin jasper connects us to the animal world, red jasper is for increased life force energy, yellow jasper inspires self-confidence and emotional energy, and green jasper is for healing and balance.

#10 CARNELIAN

Color: Red and orange

Qualities: Creativity, Courage, Assistance

Assists: Protects one's home from fire and theft and a person from psychic invasions. It stabilizes emotions, especially anger and rage.

Carnelian is one of the oldest known gemstones, with written records dating back over 4000 years. It is believed to increase passion and courage. I like to describe its vibrant energy as "the life of the party" among other crystals. It was worn by warriors and placed as amulets on the bridles of their horses for protection in battle. Carnelian is the stone of motivation and creativity. It hones the will and strengthens personal drive. It can protect against psychic invasion.

Carnelian, according to German writer and scientist Johann Wolfgang von Goethe, brought good luck to the wearer, as well as provided hope and comfort, and offered protection to them from evil. Carnelian is also believed to encourage creativity, charm, and vitality. It is particularly an excellent choice to wear to a job interview.

#11 LAPIS LAZULI

Color: Blue

Qualities: Truth, Inner Power, Organization

Assists: The awakening process for the spiritual seeker. Helps with organization and routine, enhances wisdom channels, hones focus and clarity, provides insights into dream symbology, stimulates the reasoning process, and gives access to the mysteries of the universal truths.

Lapis lazuli is said to have existed before time was born. It is reputed to enhance personal wisdom and help us gain access to sacred scriptures and ancient texts. Because it is a stone that connects the earthly and heavenly realms, it provides us with admission into the unknown mysteries and enhances our knowledge, so we can understand them.

Lapis lazuli is the stone of initiation and provides a connection between the physical kingdom and the celestial one. It is an invaluable stone for working with the energies of the realms beyond because it physically guides the human mind through altered states and back.

King Solomon was reputed to wear lapis, and legend tells us he was given a lapis ring by an angel to help him design and build his temple. The stone brings inspiration and insight to the wearer and helps with the interpretation of dreams.

Lapis lazuli balances male and female energies as in yin and yang. It represents the light of the sun and the dark of the moon. It focuses on equilibrium and balanced exchange. It revitalizes spiritual potential and encourages awareness stemming from inner wisdom.

#12 SELENITE

Color: White

Qualities: Mental Clarity, Psychic, Angels

Assists: Clarity of the mind, expansion of awareness, decreasing hesitation, and opening of the unconscious. It can reconnect one to the spiritual realms while providing insights for this lifetime. It brings clarity to business decisions by shedding a light on the inner workings. It brings out your inner goddess.

Selenite is associated with the moon, and what better example for change than the phases of the moon? This gemstone uncovers hidden meanings and brings secret agendas to the forefront. It can lead to success in business by uncovering true desires and needs because it supports mental clarity, truth, and honesty. It allows one to see deeper into a mystery and come out with a new meaning. It brings peace and harmony into the mix by dispelling any negative or unwanted energy.

Selenite has a unique quality of dissolving resistance and encourages mental flexibility. Affected by the moon and water, it creates fluid movement in all endeavors for the parties involved. It is said to enhance and accelerate spiritual development and awareness and is a direct connection to angelic realms. It keeps fear, anger, and anxiety at bay and encourages attunement to the higher self. Selenite is a beautiful stone in appearance and ability.

Summing up, the seven chakras, seven rays or rays of color are the main physical energy centers of the body. When we open them up and allow the free-flowing universal energy to course through them, we achieve a primed vessel for energy to run freely though the channels, creating harmony, balance, and connection with the divine.

CRYSTAL SPELL FOR ENDINGS

You will need:

- Incense, a diffuser, and essential oils

- Small broom

- Candles

- A small bowl of spring water

- Feathers and a wand

- A fireproof bowl

- Magic wish or flash paper

- A pen
- Crystals:
    - Jade, for love and balance
    - Black tourmaline, for absorbing negativity
    - Lapis lazuli, for new beginnings
    - Selenite, for clarity and learning
    - Carnelian, for courage
    - Red jasper, for balance
    - Turquoise, for protection against negative thoughts and feelings
    - Citrine, for confidence
    - Fluorite, for perfect order
    - Rose quartz, for forgiveness
    - Crystal quartz, for universal healing the issue

This powerful spell can apply to any type of ending, from a relationship that is no longer serving you to a job that is no longer helping you to grow. To say goodbye and close yourself off from this energy, perform the following steps:

Begin by creating your circle and placing the stones in a circle around your altar. Start the incense or diffuser. Allow the scent to permeate the air around you. Light your candles as per your ritual practice. Invite in your entities and perhaps Archangel Gabriel. Bring them together for the purpose of moving beyond someone or something with this spell.

Welcome them. State the purpose. Ask for their blessing and help.

> Entities of love and light.
>
> Be my guides this awesome night
>
> As we prepare to bid adieu
>
> To things of past, and foster new
>
> Our ritual thus begins.

Write what you want forgiven or forgotten on a piece of magic paper and place it in the burning bowl.

> There was some good that of them came
>
> And all the good I pray remain
>
> Let go of that which does not serve
>
> And with this flame I set my nerve

Strike the match and light the paper.

> The past begone in a single stroke
>
> To the heavens I commend the smoke,
>
> Now let my heart retain the good
>
> And Blessed Be as it should.

Use your tiny broom to symbolically sweep away the past. Use your wand and feather to seal the spell.

> My past does not define me,

No longer can malign me,

What's done is done

And now released

And, now at last,

I have some peace. Blessed Be.

Tap each stone and say,

Out of this, only good will sprout.

I have no fear, nor more doubt

From this day on, I'm open and free,

No strings of power over me.

The path ahead is clear and bright

I have only good within my sight. Amen and Goodnight.

Close your ceremony, and know that you have released the past, the people, the deeds, and all the emotional residue that goes with the weight of loss and sorrow. Pack up your crystals and keep them in a cloth bag next to you for the following three days to seal this release.

INITIATION INTO THE VIOLET RAY

You will need your violet or purple notebook, a purple candle, and purple pen. You will need an amethyst, a piece of selenite, and a scarf, stole, or cowl that is purple. It would be a plus if you could paint your fingernails and toes purple. Getting in touch with the seventh chakra is your key to communicating with the realms beyond. This is where we *jump the hedge*, leave the past behind us, and move upward. Jumping the hedge means placing a bet, or in horse racing, it literally indicates when the horse jumps a hedge or a barrier. In other words, we are moving from one place to another in our consciousness over the obstacles in our path.

This initial exercise is experiential and expressive. First, it is mastering the language of the universe through breath. The second is creatively expressing it.

You will need to wait for a windy (not a gale storm) day or one with a tangible breeze. (You can alternatively listen to recorded presentations of wind.)

Sit in stillness and quiet. Listen to the wind. Begin by centering yourself on your own breath. Take deep breaths until you achieve stillness within and without. Imagine the petals of a lotus unfolding. As it unfolds, feel yourself go deeper and deeper into relaxation. When you have reached the very center and core of the lotus, begin to chant AUM. Slowly, deeply, feel the vibration of the tone. Repeat a slow AUM for thirty seconds or more.

Move your attention to the wind. Envision how the wind affects flags. Picture birds flying higher and higher on the currents lifting them into dances on the wind. Picture balloons being carried off by the wind; see leaves flying through the air on the tails of the wind. What scents come in on the wind? Can you smell bread baking? The aroma of fragrant blossoms? Can you smell freshly mown grass? Do you hear voices being carried by the wind? Birdsongs?

As you become immersed in the wind, call in Archangel Gabriel. Ask him to lift you even higher and show you the next realm and the realms above it. Allow your seventh chakra to open wide and see yourself flying out of the top of your head with Gabriel at your side. Look around. What do you see? How do you feel? While you are there, place your deepest desires and wishes into the winds. They will be escorted to the right place. Visualize the violet ray and see it curving across the sky. Float, soar—enjoy your vacation in the fifth dimension. Let your face and skin begin to feel the wind in your face. Feel yourself safely descending back into your body and slipping into place. When you are there, visualize the top of your head closing the hole and returning to this dimension.

When you are safe to walk, take yourself out into the wind. Experience the breeze and the feel of it. Let it blow through your hair and cleanse your face and bathe your body with its invisible power.

Take a moment to send your wishes, blessings, and affirmations for the world, and let the wind carry them off to places far and wide. Allow them to float and rise and disappear into the ethers. When you are complete, return inside, plan your expressions, and be sure to thank Archangel Gabriel for his help and guidance. Physically and metaphorically, take your broom and jump over it on the ground. Move yourself from who you were in the past to who you are now. How does the shift feel? Let it sink in.

Now write about the wind experience in your journal. Fill the pages with your thoughts, feelings, and visions. Did you meet anyone along the way? What did you learn? Is this an exercise you want to repeat? Write down your desires, what you claimed and record the blessing you sent out on the wind. Next, prepare to make a creative expression of your experience with the wind. Will you paint this experience, write a poem, record a song, sculpt a shape, make a piece of clothing, knit a cape, bake a cake? What will your expression of this experience look like and how will it manifest? Do that now. When you have completed it, take a photo, and print it out so you can put a copy of it in your journal.

This is the last ray you have to earn and master. Have you been able to incorporate the rays into your solar plexus? Is there anything you want to review? Describe how you are feeling right now.

As you investigate all seven rays and complete their respective initiations, you should feel the change in your personal power and your magic. You should have a renewed sense of the sacred. Remember that you, as a Rainbow Witch and a human being, matter so much to the future of this world: you can become a force of good that can overtake any evil. Take the Rainbow Witch pledge below, and then I would ask you to seek out other Rainbow Witches around the world. The movement will grow, and our strength will be apparent. Be on the lookout for the good in the world, which will show up in all of the vibrant colors of the rainbow. Everything you were waiting for is happening now.

PLEDGE OF THE RAINBOW WITCH

In my heart the rainbow grows.

I embrace the colors and make them my own.

I pledge only good will come from my hands.

I recognize the power in magic.

I pledge to always be true to my calling.

Never stray from my resolve.

And I accept my place as a master,

in the magical realms of rainbow colors.

I promise to put my gifts to good use

and to spread the message of Love.

Blessed Be.

The world is in your hands. Congratulations, Rainbow Witch!

CONCLUSION

As the spiritual world moves toward oneness and unity, it makes sense that witches unite, too. Why not become a Rainbow Witch and incorporate all the good there is in every practice? See your practice through the lens of a prism and incorporate all the colors of the rainbow and live fully, abundantly, and in living color. You have read about their qualities and empowerments, and you have heard wiser sages add their thoughts. It's up to you to carry on this mission. Studying the colored rays takes time. I find that every year, every practice brings new insights about the color. Your instincts will be heightened, and you will see colors in a different way now that you have studied them and worked with them. I'm sure you will find new ways to deepen their use. When the students surpass the master, that is a sign of success.

Take these rays with you into the world and keep them active in your life and heart. Share them with others, but make sure they do the same work and processes as you have done. The rainbow is nothing to be played with, it is to be used sacredly.

Remember that you are divinely loved and cosmically cherished. May you feel as great as you truly are and always have been. Never be shy about taking a bow and feeling the rainbow of love in a radiant canopy overhead. Blessed Be.

APPENDIX A

Tree Correspondences

The chart below lists trees with qualities that lend themselves to the creation of wands and other spellwork. When crafting a wand, choose wood from one of these trees that possesses the qualities you cherish most.

Tree Name	Spiritual Aspect
Acacia	Divine Authority, Spiritual Leadership, Immortality, Psychic Connection, Protection
Alder	Balanced male-female energy, Rebirth, Self-Regulation, Healing
Almond	Beauty, Fertility, Goodness, Energy, Grief, Hidden Treasures, Hope, Clairvoyance
Apple	Winning, Conquest, Ultimate Prize, Golden Apple, Happiness
Ash	Strength, Power, Divine Connection, Authority, Protection
Aspen	Communication with the Next World, Protection from Spiritual Harm, Eloquence, Peace, Anti-theft
Avocado	Rebirth, Lust, Beauty, Ultimate Love
Banyan	Immortality, Longevity, Death, Hermit
Baobab	Ancient Awareness, Divine Communication, Blessings, Earth Wisdom, Knowledge, Spiritual Power, Sustenance
Beech	Protection of the Heart, Trust, New Growth, Unlocking Wisdom, Nurturing, Letting Go of Old Ways, Knowledge
Birch	Renewal, Protection, New Beginnings
Boswellia	Protection, Healing, Consecration, Purification

Tree Name	Spiritual Aspect
Cedar	Strength, Longevity, Eternity, Gateway to Higher Realms, Prosperity
Cherry	New Awakenings, Rebirth, Love, Romance, Going Forward
Chestnut	Life, Fertility, Birth Sustenance
Coconut	Tree of Life, Food, Shelter, Liquid Nourishment, Purity, Healing
Coffee	Emotions, Changes, Transformation, Friendship, Balance
Cottonwood	Hope, Healing, Transformation, Ancient Wisdom, Ancestors
Cypress	Immortality, Protection, Longevity, Past Lives
Dogwood	Secrets, Loyalty, Protection, Wishes
Elder	Transformation, Death, Regeneration, Healing, Protection
Elm	Nobility, Open-Mindedness, Communication, Relationships, Feminine Power
Eucalyptus	Division Between Heaven and Earth, Purification, Cleansing, Healing
Fig	Fertility, Protection, Sacredness, Enlightenment, Strength
Fir	Protection, Spiritual Honesty, Truth, Youth, Vitality, Immortality
Ginkgo	Magic, Longevity, Fertility, Prosperity
Hawthorne	Renewal, Fertility, Cleansing, Married Love, Balance of Opposites, Looking Deeper, Communication with the Spirit World
Hazel	Wisdom, Chastity, Spirituality, Prophecy, Healing, Fertility
Hemlock	Vulnerability, Yin, Introspection, Shelter, Inner Knowing, Radical Transformation.
Holly	Unconditional Love, Sacred, Reincarnation, Protection Against Evil, Material Fortune

Tree Name	Spiritual Aspect
Jacaranda	Wisdom, Wealth, Good Luck, Rebirth
Juniper	Purification of Home, Funerary Rites, Banishment of Evil Spells, Undoing of Curses, Protection
Lemon	Fertility, Uplifting, Happiness, Joy, Cleansing, Love, Light, Divination
Linden	Tranquility, Love, Longevity, Prophecy
Mahogany	Safety, Strength, Protection, Magic
Magnolia	Adaptability, Healing, Love, Loyalty, Rest
Maple	Development, Perseverance, Vitality, Humility, Harmony
Mulberry	Balance, Defense, Bravery, Wisdom
Myrtle	Love, Longevity, Strength, Stability, Enterprising
Neem	Purification, Universal Healing
Oak	Strength, Authority, Cosmic Knowledge, Balancing, Fertility, Money, Healing
Olive	Peace, Wisdom, Fertility, Prosperity, Health, Victory, Stability, Fidelity
Orange	Generosity, Wisdom, Honor, Chastity, Purity
Palm	Victory, Triumphant, Peace, Eternal Life, Resurrection, Male Strength
Pine	Immortality, Eternity, Fertility, Enlightenment, Regeneration
Redwood	Longevity, Strength, Invincibility, Vital Heaven and Earth Connection, Eternity
Rowan	Psychic Powers, Fairy Tree, Death, Rebirth, Protection Against Enchantment
Sassafras	Prosperity, Healing, Tenacity, Whimsy, Changes, Fairness, Triple Goddess

Tree Name	Spiritual Aspect
Willow	Enchantment, Immortality Creativity, Protection, Flexibility, Lunar Attunement, Moon Cycles, Healing
Yew	Yggdrasil, Meaning of Life, Nine World, Rebirth, Resilience, Other World Travel, Purification, Death, Transportation to the Afterlife, Guardian of the Underworld.

Many prefer to work with a wand made of natural wood. It accepts the vibration of your arm and resonates within the cells of the wood. I don't recommend anything made of plastic, but a gemstone wand might suit your tastes. Whatever you choose, please keep it from nature.

People may make wands of plastic and people-made substances. Those are fine for playtime, but I do not agree that they work all that well in true magic.

If you find a tree and wish to have a branch for your wand, please ask the tree's permission before you take a branch. Offer a blessing, a sincere request, if you receive permission, cut the branch off with one movement using a sharp knife and heal the wound of the tree with tea water. Be sure to leave a gift for the tree behind and always offer your gratitude.

When I found my wand, I asked permission, left a gift, healed the tree, and a few months later, I brought the finished wand back to the tree and left behind a photo of it for the tree to enjoy.

Find a wand you love. Make a wand you cherish. Use your wand only for good intentions and you will be a successful healer. Always keep your wand in a sacred place or a special box away from inquisitive children or dogs seeking a new bone. Namaste.

Rest well. Be blessed.

Celtic Tree Birth Signs

The Celts believed that a people born under a certain "tree" sign would have certain personality traits and strengths. Have a look at the trees below and find your birth month to determine what tree you resonate with, according to the day you were born. Also included are the essential oils and gemstones related to your Celtic Tree sign. The Celtic year always began at Yule.

If you were born **December 24 through January 20,** your tree would be the **Birch** (*Betula pendula* Roth) and you would be known as **The Achiever.**

> **PERSONALITY:**
>
> + Highly driven
>
> + A motivator
>
> + Tough and reliant like the birch tree
>
> + Cool-headed and naturally confident (born ruler)
>
> + Skilled leader
>
> + Brighten any space with charm and quick wit
>
> **ESSENTIAL OIL:** Birch Essential Oil (Betula lenta) extracted from the pulverized bark of the birch tree.

If you were born **January 21 through February 17,** your tree would be the **Rowan** (*Sorbus aucuparia* L.) also known as Mountain Ash, and you would be known as **The Thinker.**

> **PERSONALITY:**
>
> + Visionary

- Keen mind

- Original, creative

- Thought of as aloof yet burning inside with passion.

- Ability to transform

- Highly influential in a quiet manner

ESSENTIAL OIL: Lavender (*Lavandula angustifolia*)

If you were born **February 18 through March 17,** your tree would be the **Ash** (*Fraxinus excelsior* L.), not related to the mountain ash, and you would be known as **The Enchanter.** Ash is related to the olive and lilac family (*Oleaceae*).

PERSONALITY:

- Imaginative, intuitive, naturally artistic

- Constant inner motion

- You love art, science, writing, poetry, and spirituality

- Seen as reclusive, but just immersed in your own world

- Constantly self-renewing

- Unaffected by what others think about you

ESSENTIAL OIL: Lilac (*Syringa vulgaris*)

If you were born **March 18 through April 14**, your tree would be the Alder (*Alnus glutinosa*) and you would be known as **The Trailblazer**.

PERSONALITY:

+ Charming, gregarious

+ Mingle easily with people

+ Gets along with everyone and is liked by all.

+ Highly confident with strong faith in self

+ Highly focused, dislikes waste or fluff

+ Motivated by action.

ESSENTIAL OIL: Ginger (*Zingiber officinale*)

If you were born **April 15 through May 12**, your tree would be the Willow (*Salix alba* L.) and you would be known as **The Observer**.

PERSONALITY:

+ Highly psychic

+ Connected to the moon and mysticism

+ Keen understanding of cycles

+ Intelligent

+ Knowledgeable on many subjects

+ Acutely perceptive

ESSENTIAL OIL: Roman chamomile
(*Chamaemelum nobile*)

If you were born **May 13 through June 9,** your tree would be the **Hawthorn** (*Crataegus monogyna* Jacq.) and you would be known as **The Illusionist.**

PERSONALITY:

+ Excellent listener

+ Natural curiosity

+ Sense of humor

+ Sees the big picture

+ Has amazing insight

+ Gives self very little credit.

ESSENTIAL OIL: Hawthorn Berry
(*Crataegus oxycanthus*)

If you were born **June 10 through July 7,** your tree would be the **Oak** (*Quercus robur* L.) and you would be known as **The Stabilizer.**

PERSONALITY:

+ Positive

+ Confident

+ All works out for the good

+ Spokesperson for the underdog

+ Has a deep respect for ancestors

+ Makes a good teacher

ESSENTIAL OIL: Oakmoss (*Evernia prunastri*) or Bergamot (*Citrus bergamia*)

If you were born **July 8 through August 4,** your tree would be **Holly** (*Ilex aquifolium* L.) and you would be known as **The Ruler.**

PERSONALITY:

+ Leader

+ Goal oriented

+ Vigilant—seldom defeated

+ Generous, kind, intelligent

+ Self-confident

+ Overcome obstacles easily

ESSENTIAL OIL: Red Thyme (*Thymus vulgaris*)

If you were born **August 5 through September 1,** your tree would be the **Hazel** (*Corylus avellana L*) and you would be known as **The Knower.**

PERSONALITY:

+ Well informed

+ Genuinely smart

+ Eye for details

- Likes order

- Ability to retain information

    ESSENTIAL OIL: Hazelnut Carrier Oil
    (*Corylus avellana*)

If you were born **September 2 through September 29,** your tree would be **Vine** (*Vitis vinifera L*) and you would be known as **The Equalizer.**

PERSONALITY:

- Changeable and unpredictable

- Can see both sides and can be indecisive

- Loves food, wine, music, art

- Charming, elegant, classy

- Has the Midas touch

- Publicly appreciated and esteemed

    ESSENTIAL OIL: Frankincense (*Boswellia carteri*)

If you were born **September 30 through October 27,** your tree would be **Ivy** (*Hedera helix L.*) and you would be known as **The Survivor.**

PERSONALITY:

- Sharp intellect

- Compassionate and loyal

- Always lend a helping hand

+ Silent endurance, soulful grace

+ Deeply spiritual

+ Soft spoken and charismatic

ESSENTIAL OIL: Rose absolute (*Rosa x damascene*)

If you were born **October 28 through November 24,** your tree would be **Reed** (*Phragmites australis* (Cav.) Trin. Ex Steudel) and you would be known as **The Inquisitor.**

PERSONALITY:

+ Deep digger into the heart of the matter

+ Discovers hidden truths

+ Keeper of secrets—honorable

+ Storyteller and story lover

+ Detective, historian, archaeologist

ESSENTIAL OIL: Myrrh (*Commiphora myrrha*)

If you were born **November 25 through December 23,** your tree would be the **Elder** (*Sambucus nigra* L.) and you would be known as **The Seeker.**

PERSONALITY:

+ Deeply thoughtful, philosophical

+ Extrovert and yet somewhat withdrawn

+ Considerate of others

- ✦ Brutally honest
- ✦ Extremely helpful

ESSENTIAL OIL: Rosemary (*Rosmarinus officinalis*)

The purpose of the Celtic Tree birth sign in our day is to let the trees reveal something about us to ourselves and how our gifts are akin to a magnificent being in nature. Trees are charged with life force just as we are, and they have a lot to teach us about the macrocosm and the microcosm we call life. They teach us from the heart, from the very essence of who they are. They do not teach us through books, or lectures, but from their souls.

There were other trees that were also sacred to the Celts. They were Alder, Apple, Ash, Birch, Blackthorn, Broom, Cedar, Elder, Elm, Fir, Furze (Gorse), Hawthorn, Hazel, Holly, Juniper, Mistletoe, Oak, Pine, Rowan, Willow, and Yew.

APPENDIX B

Magical Alphabets

Rainbow Witches work with symbols and hidden meanings in ordinary things. Our ancestors created alphabets and ways to communicate with entities beyond the earth as well as in their communities. Here are some systems of ancient writing that may be useful to you.

THE RUNES

Originally the runes were ancient lettering used to write in the Germanic and Scandinavian languages preceding the adoption of the Latin alphabet. That is a clinical definition of them. The other definition is that they were given to the god Odin by the goddess Freya, the goddess of love and known for her magic. Odin had hung himself upside down on the Yew tree so he could obtain wisdom. On the ninth day, just as he was dying, the runes were given to him, and he lived. That's because the magical goddess whispered the runes to him that were deeply held secrets and communications from the spirit world into the real world.

The Nordic peoples were highly spiritual and lived by strict codes of life and conduct. Women were equals, could own land and hold positions of power, and often fought next to the men in battle. Marriage was renewed each year if both parties agreed. They often went to the mountains to sacrifice to their gods, Odin, Frigg, Thor, Loki, Balder, Hod, Heimdall, and Tyr. The Nordic peoples were fierce in their beliefs and their practices because they had to endure the bitterly cold winters and to bear a wintery land without heat, light, or crops.

The runes were two things. They were letters with which to communicate with others, which soldiers used as warning signs—they would leave them in the forest for the warriors who came behind them. They warned of dangers ahead with stick-runes bound together with reeds. Secondly, they were signs of divination and messages from the gods that could predict the future and foretell of drought and famine as well as prosperity and bounty.

If you choose to work with runes, please learn more about them. They are complex. Every writer has a different opinion; the best way to work with them is to learn their names and read about their meanings then and now. What was important to the Norse may not apply to you today, but the principles still hold. For example, *Fehu* means "cattle" from the runes. In the past, cattle were a symbol of wealth. So today, the rune would mean wealth in the form of money, relationships, well-being, family, and all you hold dear as personal treasure in your heart. A great online source for information about the individual runes and their meanings is runesecrets.com.

THE CELTIC OGHAM

The Ogham is an alphabet used by the Celts in 600 BCE during the Roman occupation. However, some historians date it back to the fall of The Tower of Babel in 2200 BCE. Various scholars argue that the symbols were created from the Greek alphabet and others claim from the Latin. The most popular answer is Latin because that's what the Romans spoke when they came to the islands. However, it could be Phoenician, too.

The Ogham is an alphabet consisting of twenty-five letters which were inscribed in wood and stone and bisected by a straight line. It was called *Beith-luis-nin*, referring to Birch, Rowan, and Ash. The letters are divided into groups known as aicmi or families. The original Ogham comprises four groups of five letters for a total of twenty letters. At some later date, another group of five letters, called forfeda, was added. These groupings reflect the counting system traditionally used in Ireland, which emphasized sets of five, twenty, and fifty. See pages 192–193 for the division of the groups.

Not everyone could read the Ogham. It was an art and a practice reserved for the bards who were the wisemen, sorcerers, musicians, astrologers, and poets. It is interesting to note that there were four levels of bards in Britain and Ireland. The bard was on the lowest rung and the filidh was the highest. It was the norm to spend three or four years at each level of poetry in the bardic schools before moving up. The fifth level was the filidh, and these bards were accomplished enough to be the king's official poet. When we use the word *poet*, we mean they could do many things that included interpreting Brehon Law, the ancient Celtic system of social government, advising about court and tribal matters, national concerns, all of which was answered in different poetic formats. These bards and filidhs mastered the Ogham script and could read and write it effortlessly.

There is a story from the tribal wars that tells of one king coming up a hill to attack another king. The king under attack inscribed an Ogham on a circle of wood and tossed it in the approaching king's path. The aggressor king could not read what it said and called for his filidh to interpret the symbols for him. It took a few days for him to arrive. If the message was good, he needed to know that, If the message was negative, he needed to know that too before proceeding with his attack. I don't know the outcome of the incident, but for our entertainment purposes wouldn't it be fun to assume that the invading king changed his mind and went home after waiting for so many days to find out what was written on the wood? After this incident, bards traveled with the army when it went to war.

If very few people could read and interpret the Ogham, what was it used for? Many things apparently. It was used for creating documents, for marking land, for determining the boundaries of a kingdom, for tombstones, for memorials, and for recording history for future generations.

Medieval historians associated Ogham inscriptions with secret messages, magic, and Pagan lore. Interestingly, Ogham was never used for literary purposes. It was limited to short texts only.

The earliest examples of Ogham letters were carved onto large columnar stones. The script writer began chiseling on the lower left side of the stone and worked their way up. Ogham text is read from the bottom of the left-hand edge of the stone moving upward to the top of the stone, then across the top edge and downward to the bottom right-hand corner of the stone, designed to be the exact way to climb a tree, bottom to top.

Each letter of the Ogham script was named for a tree. The Celts were intertwined with the tree kingdom because trees were regarded as repositories of memory and lore and alive with the presence of spirit beings who lived within the tree. As such, trees were deemed sacred in Celtic Britain and Ireland.

It was thought that stone carvings preceded the wooden carvings or staves; however, looking at the evolution of nature, and since wood disintegrates over time, it was possible, several scholars pose, that the wooden imprints decayed leaving only the carved stone versions for us to investigate. We do know that the Ogham alphabet was used for communication, as a coded language, probably so the Celts could keep secrets from the Romans, and the alphabet was carved into wood, bark, leather, and stones and were used for sacred rituals and divination.

If you find yourself attracted to this tree-based system, you can find Ogham divination tools on the Internet and various sites you can search on the web. Best of all, you can make your own, which is probably the most fun.

DIVINATION MEANING FOR EACH OGHAM SYMBOL

AICME OF BEITH

B is for Beith—**Birch**	(Cleansing, hope, new beginnings)
L is for Luis—**Rowan**	(Protection, clear vision, psychic connection)
F is for Feàrn—**Alder**	(Encouragement, self-confidence, shield)
S is for Suil—**Willow**	(Harmony, balance, flexibility)
N is for Nuin—**Ash**	(Courage, strength, focus)

AICME OF HUATH

H is for Huath—**Hawthorn**	(Heart, beauty, love)
D is for Dair/Duir—**Oak**	(Strength, loyalty, leadership)
T is for Teine—**Holly**	(Boundaries, protection, empathy)
C is for Coll—**Hazel**	(Wisdom, inspiration, insight)
Q is for Quert—**Apple**	(Wholeness, attraction, vitality)

AICME OF MUIN

M is for Muin—**Blackberry**	(Harvest, abundance, wealth)
G is for Gort—**Ivy**	(Friendship, connection, support)
R is for Ruis—**Elder**	(Endings & beginnings, yin-yang)
Ng is for Ngetal—**Reed**	(Direction, purpose, responsibility)
St is for Straif—**Blackthorn**	(Power, magical protection, positivity)

AICME OF AILM

A is for Ailm—**Elm or Fir**	(Values, warrior, loyalty)
O is for Onn—**Gorse**	(Life force, solar power, prosperity)

U is for Ur—**Heather**	(Love, passion, desire)
E is for Eadha—**Poplar**	(Success, transformation, endurance)
I is for Idha—**Yew**	(Ancestral wisdom, immortality, other-world connection)

FIFTH AICME

The Fifth Aicme is an additional section in the Ogham alphabet.

Éa for Eabhadh—**Meaning unknown**

Ór for Oir—**Gold**

Ui for Uileann—**Elbow**

Ia for Ifin—**Pine**

Ae for Eamhancholl—**"groan of a sick person"**

OTHER SYMBOLS

The below are other symbols that are not part of the standard alphabet.

P for Peith (soft birch)—**a variant of Beith**

E for Eite (feather)—**marks start of texts**

S for Spás (space)—**Indicates a space**

E for Eite thuthail (reversed feather)—**marks end of texts**

FIRST AICME

T	TT	TTT	TTTT	TTTTT
Beith	Luis	Fern	Sail	Nion
B	L	F	S	N

SECOND AICME

⊥	⊥⊥	⊥⊥⊥	⊥⊥⊥⊥	⊥⊥⊥⊥⊥
Uath	Dair	Tinne	Coll	Ceirt
H	D	T	C	Q

THIRD AICME

⧸	⫻	⫻⫻	⫻⫻⫻	⫻⫻⫻⫻
Muin	Gort	Ngeadal	Straif	Ruis
M	G	NG	Z	R

FOURTH AICME

+	++	+++	++++	+++++
Ailm	Onn	Ur	Eadhadh	Iodhadh
A	O	U	E	I

FIFTH AICME

✸	◈	🖰	✖	▦	═
Eabhad	Or	Uilleann	Ifin	Emhanchooll	Peith
EA	O	UI	IA	AE	P

OTHER SYMBOLS

	⅄	—	≺	
	Start	Space	End	

MAGICAL PROPERTIES OF TREES

+ **Alder:** banishing, divination, healing, protection, psychic intuition, resurrection

+ **Apple:** underworld, love, healing, goddess, garden, immortality

+ **Ash:** balance, communication, fertility, harmony, healing, knowledge, love divination, prophecy, protection from drowning, transition

+ **Aspen:** ancestry, astral planes, eloquence, endurance, healing, money, peace, rebirth, success

+ **Bamboo:** fortune, flexibility, longevity, luck, protection

- **Banyan:** abundance, divine connection, immortality, longevity, luck, protection

- **Beech:** ancestry, creativity, friendship, protection, second sight, wisdom

- **Birch:** birth, blessings, creativity, crafting, fertility, goddess, healing, inspiration, love, protection, renewal

- **Blackthorn:** authority, protection, strength, truth

- **Bottlebrush:** abundance, banishing, energy, fertility, love, purification

- **Camphor:** banishing, cleansing, divination, exorcism, healing, love, lust, prophecy

- **Cedar:** balance, dreams, healing, immortality, longevity, prosperity, protection, purification, wisdom

- **Cypress:** grieving, healing, longevity, protection, solace

- **Elder:** blessings, creativity, fairies, good fortune, healing, magic, prosperity, protection, sleep, transition

- **Elm:** birth, compassion, grounding, healing, intuition, love, protection, rebirth, wisdom

- **Fig:** ancient ancestry, divination, enlightenment, fertility, good luck, love, prosperity

- **Fir:** birth, far-sightedness, protection, prosperity, rebirth, vitality

- **Gorse:** divination, fertility, prosperity, protection

- **Hawthorn:** ancestry, cleansing, fairies, family, fertility, happiness, love, marriage, prosperity, protection, purification, wisdom

- **Hazel:** creativity, divination, fertility, healing, knowledge, luck, protection, wisdom

- **Heather:** changes, healing, luck, passion, protection, spirituality

- **Hemlock:** cleansing, mysteries, shadow work

- **Hickory:** abundance, discipline, flexibility, kindness, protection, strength, transformation

- **Holly:** courage, death, divinity, healing, luck, protection, rebirth, unity

- **Juniper:** cleansing, healing, love, protection

- **Magnolia:** clarity, dreams, love, protection, truth

- **Maple:** abundance, communication, divination, grounding, love, money, wisdom

- **Mimosa:** happiness, love, protection, purification, sensitivity

- **Oak:** ancestry, fertility, health, luck, prosperity, protection, strength, success, wisdom

- **Palm:** abundance, fertility, flexibility, healing, potency, protection

- **Pine:** abundance, emotions, fertility, good luck, healing, immortality, love, prosperity, protection, purification, regeneration

- **Rowan:** blessings, centering, expression, fertility, grounding, healing, luck, music, protection, strength, writing

- **Sequoia:** enlightenment, eternity, growth, valor, wisdom

- **Spruce:** enlightenment, grounding, healing, intuition, protection, versatility

- **Willow:** birth, fertility, flexibility, grieving, healing, intuition, knowledge, motherhood, protection, relationships, wisdom, wishes

- **Witch Hazel:** healing, protection

- **Yew:** ancestry, death, divination, flexibility, immortality, rebirth, strength

Reprinted courtesy Kitty Fields, Otherworldly Oracle

APPENDIX C

Directional Correspondences

We mentioned in the red ray chapter that Archangel Uriel was the guardian of the direction north. Have you ever wondered if you have a special direction and what that might mean? Interestingly enough, it does matter. Let's have a look at how and why.

Directions are based on cardinal points. Cardinal points are directions agreed upon by civilizations worldwide to make it easier to communicate and retain global order. The four cardinal directions are north, south, east, and west, based on the rising and setting of the sun as the central reference point. Since Earth rotates from west to east, the sun appears to rise in the east and set in the west, even in the southern hemisphere.

We know that every person is born with certain qualities and talents and cultivates even more of them as they mature. The early Celts believed the cardinal points on the earth support and define those same qualities in people. In this scenario, east is not better than west and south does not trump north. No direction rules because they're all equal in importance. Knowing which direction you are helps in determining how you will practice your witchcraft.

North people are good leaders. They are task-based, set goals, are born assertive, and have an independent spirit. Northers can make decisions quickly, adore competition, and have a natural born air of confidence.

People with a South direction love whatever process they are involved in. They prefer diplomacy to contention and make good team players. They are listeners, excel in sensitivity for others, and welcome differing opinions with understanding. They possess the gift of unlimited patience, are generous, and always offer a helping hand. They work very well in groups and make others comfortable.

If you are a planner and a stickler for details, you have East in your bones. You analyze everything, are highly organized, razor sharp, logical, easily focus on the task at hand, and can be somewhat of a perfectionist. You are industrious and love structure in all you do.

And then there's the wild, wild West. You have walked on many a wild side and are no stranger to taking risks, yet are highly creative, intensely talented at innovation, and can see the big picture. You are spontaneous, energetic, enthusiastic, and free-spirited like a kite in the wind.

Do you identify with any of those directions? Which one describes you? If you don't feel a fit, yet perhaps you are a combination of two or three. Which one is most dominant? Let's consider.

NE. If you are part North and part East you might be conducive to hard work, are accountable, productive, and trustworthy to the core. You always finish the task at hand, catch errors, and face life seriously.

NW. Blending North and West makes you a player. You move fast, talk big dreams, sign right up for the action, confidently take risks, have a daring quality about you, and are never afraid of change. You're one of those people who welcomes change and loves what it leaves in its wake. It is always all good with the Northwesterner.

SE. You probably were teacher's pet because you prefer to follow set rules, are a good listener, and usually act conservatively and with caution. You don't like to rattle the status quo and are methodical as you take life slow and easy. Change isn't your best friend because and it takes a long time for you to adapt to it.

SW. Being from the South and the West, you are very social and live to motivate and inspire others, but you shirk pressure, and at the same time are highly adaptable and would do anything to avoid deadlines whenever possible.

APPENDIX D

Symbols for Rainbow Witchcraft

You have learned about some symbols that can be specifically applied to the seven rays in the chapters of this book. However, peruse the paragraphs below if you'd like to add more to your practice.

The numbers six and ten are important in witchcraft. Six represents equilibrium and ten signifies completion.

The mystical rose is the symbol of divine love. The heart is the true symbol of the soul.

The yin-yang symbol represents the center of the universe that is always in movement, always shifting, and always changing, and that activity occurs because there is a little of the yin in the yang and a little of the yang in the yin. One completes the other and cannot exist without its opposite. This is the basis for the cosmology of the ancient Chinese and the foundation of the Tao.

Each side depends on the other for its life because one cannot function without the other. It is only in working together that they make up the whole.

The Sun, the male energy, and power are represented by this symbol, ☉

The Moon's feminine energy is represented by this symbol, ☾

Next, we'll look at The Eye of Horus because it was believed that his right eye was the Sun and his left Eye the Moon. This symbol represents protection and prosperity. 𓂀

The symbols of life come in many forms and from many cultures. The Seed of the Universe, ✿

The Spiral of Life, and the ancient Egyptian Symbol of Life, the Ankh. ☥

The Celts described life as a spiral, so we have, ◎

Another symbol of life for the ancient Celts was the triskele (⚛). It is said to be the oldest symbol of spirituality. It represents the number three, the number meaning divinity, and since many things happen in a pattern of three, it also gives meaning to the phrase *third time's a charm*. This is the reason spells and blessing are repeated three times.

The Celts used a single line to make a knot to represent the meaning of eternity and protection against any person or thing that might wish to penetrate the well-being or magic of the person wearing or using the symbol.

The Evil Eye (◉), worldwide recognition of protection against harm.

The ancient symbol for success (↯) is always wonderful to use in magical ceremonies or spells because it bodes victory in magical workings.

Not used that often, but sometimes wanted for magical spells, this symbol (⋏) represents death, but it mostly means ending old ways so a better way can arise. Its meaning is much broader than mortality.

Many witches like to use the Horned God, the Besom (broom), the Owl, and other symbols from ancient cultures. Help yourself to whatever feels good. Or you can can make your own symbols, called sigils; these are the most powerful and effective spell work of all. See page 105 for a discussion of sigils.

USING THE SYMBOLS IN A SPELL OR RITUAL

When setting up your altar, decide what kind of a spell or ritual you are going to perform.

Choose a card, Sun, Moon, or Eye of Horus if you are performing a spell for another person. (Sun is male, Moon is female, and Eye of Horus is non-binary, them, or blended gender identity.) Or choose a card for yourself that represents your identity expression if you are working for yourself.

Next, choose the card #6 to establish you are beginning. Call in your guides, entities, angels, or helpers. Place the triskele card on top of the #6 card to establish this spell is being said for alignment with divine purpose.

> Today begins another spell,
>
> For good results that end so well
>
> We bless this space for all to see
>
> The power of love that shines in me
>
> I speak it out for all to hear
>
> Across the sky, far and near
>
> That what I claim will manifest
>
> Success is met and we are blessed.

At this point, state what it is you are asking for or stating. Use words that frame your ask as if it has already manifested. Use cards as you ask and place them on top, facing up, on your stack. Always state your spell three times.

Use the yin-yang card if you seek balance.

Use the rose card if you seek love.

Use the Seed of the Universe and the Spiral of Life, either Egyptian or Celtic, for a baby or for fertility.

Use the triskele card if you seek health.

Use the Celtic Knot if you seek protection or longevity.

Use the Evil Eye or Mati if you seek protection from a curse or ill-wisher.

Use your wand to tap the stack of cards three times. Seal it with a crystal, smoke, or a feather, or all three.

I release this wish into your care

Naysayers now beware

This wish is sealed with love and prayer

Now vanishes into cosmic air

To become the truth of what we spoke

To greet the stars on wings of smoke.

Place the success card on top of the pile, tap your wand three times.

Our job today is sealed and done

Our wish has chosen to become

Manifest for all to see.

Our final words are Blessed Be.

As you say those last words, place the completion card #10 on the pile. Tap it three times with your wand and turn the pile of cards over so only the orange back side is showing. The spell is complete. Please close your ceremony and thank your guides, masters, angels, and helpers.

APPENDIX E

Which Witch?

Here is an easy reference to review as you move through the seven rays of the rainbow. Although a Rainbow Witch's magic is all her own, it derives its magic from all-encompassing love and universal connection. Therefore you may wish to research and integrate practices and beliefs from other schools of witchcraft that may complement your own practices. Each of the chapters in this book contains a few ways to view the craft that may be useful to you. Here is a ray-by-ray list and a brief description of each.

UNDER THE RED RAY

+ Chaos Witch—a witch who places faith in themselves with no attachment to strict rituals, deities, dogma, or any other binding object of faith.

+ Dianic Witch—a witch who is a modern Pagan using the goddess tradition for the purpose of female empowerment. (Diana the warrior goddess.)

+ Fire Witch—a witch who works with the element of fire, coals, wood, and the concept of purification by flame.

+ Gardnerian Witch—a witch following a highly structured Wiccan version founded by Gerald Gardner.

- Hereditary Witch—a witch who was born into witchcraft and learns through generational handed-down teachings.

- Tech Witch—a witch who uses digital devices for their practice and magic.

- Traditional Witch—a witch who follows traditional lore and practices from the British Isles and is not influenced by any of the modern witch movements.

Under the Orange Ray

- Alexandrian Witch—a witch who practices a form of Wicca with rituals based on the Hermetic Qabalah and Enochian magic founded in the 1960s in the UK.

- Chthonioi Witch—a witch who practices based on the Greek gods and goddesses in the Alexandrian tradition, founded in 1974.

- Hellenic Witch—a Pagan witch who uses the power of the gods and goddesses of the Greek Pantheon.

- Left-Handed Witch—a witch who breaks taboos and rejects set moral standards.

- Norse Witch—a witch who uses traditional Norse sorcery and the deities of Odin and Freya to foretell and shape the future. Also known as seidhr.

- Sun Witch—a witch who uses solar power, myth, and legend in their practice.

- Urban Witch—a witch who adapts her magic and love of nature to the intricacies and diverse spiritual ecosystem that is their city

UNDER THE YELLOW RAY

- Correllian Witch—a witch who practices Pagan witchcraft with Native American practices added.

- Eclectic Witch—a witch who can follow strict guidelines or incorporate different traditions into their work, similar to the Chaos Witch.

- Luciferian Witch—a witch who sees Lucifer as the angel of light; an enlightener, questions authority, and is similar to the Left-Handed path.

- Neo-Pagan Witch—an umbrella witch using the newer forms of witchcraft such as Wicca and Gardnerian.

- Secular Witch—a witch who uses spells, crystals, candles without connecting to a deity or a higher being. Non-religious.

- Wiccan Witch—a witch who follows the practices of Gerald Brousseau Gardner (1884–1964) based on a reverence for nature, practice of magic, and the worship of the Goddess.

Under the Green Ray

+ Axis Mundi Witch—A witch who believes there is a central pillar that connects heaven and earth.

+ Celtic Witch—a witch who concentrates on ancient Celtic deities, mythology, and rituals, and practices earth magic.

+ Cottage Witch—a witch focused on the home, with some Green Witch and Kitchen Witch practices included.

+ Faery Witch—a witch who works with the fae and grounded in Scottish and Celtic practices.

+ Green Witch—a witch who is deeply connected to the earth and also known as a Forest Witch.

+ Hearth Witch—a witch who is part herbal and part magical healing, similar to the Kitchen Witch, who practices from the home.

+ Kitchen Witch—similar to the Cottage Witch or a Hearth Witch, but with a focus on the kitchen and products therein.

Under the Blue Ray

+ British Traditional Witch—a witch who practices with the superstitions and spells from the British Isles.

- Egyptian Witch—a witch who focuses on the Egyptian Deities and magic.

- Elemental Witch—a witch who works with the five elements of earth, water, fire, air, and spirit.

- Folk Witch—a witch who follows a similar path to British witchcraft using their magic for practical purposes and passed down through generations. Also known as "cunning folk" or wise people.

- Music Witch—a witch who uses the magic and mystery of music as the basis of their practice.

- Sea Witch—a witch with strong ties to water, especially the ocean, who uses gifts from the ocean and beach in their practice.

- Sigil Witch—a witch, also known as a "Word Witch," who uses sigils and words throughout their magic.

UNDER THE INDIGO RAY

- Ancestral Witch—a witch who honors their ancestors year-round by connecting with them spiritually and magically.

- Animist Witch—a witch who sees the universe as a living entity with no difference between animals, people, or material objects.

+ Augury Witch—a witch who divines omens, signs, and symbols.

+ Ceremonial Witch—a witch dedicated to ceremonies and rituals calling on specific beings for their magic.

+ Divination Witch—a witch who uses many occult methods to predict the future or to receive information about the present circumstances.

+ Shamanic Witch—a witch who uses the powers of the other side along with the magic and medicine of plants and animals.

+ Solitary Witch—a witch of any type who prefers to practice alone without a coven.

Under the Violet Ray

+ Angel Witch—a witch who works with angels.

+ Cosmic Witch—a witch who uses the placement of the planets, moons, and stars for their practice.

+ Crystal Witch—a witch who uses crystals and crystal power for spells, rituals, and practices.

+ Hedge Witch—a witch who "jumps the hedge," meaning moves easily between the earthly and astral planes.

+ Lunar/Moon Witch—a witch who uses the cycles of the moon as the basis for their magic.

+ Right-Handed Witch—a witch who believes in divine union and works the path for reunification with the divine.

+ Swamp Witch—a witch who has disdain for social norms and prefers mud-caked shoes. This witch rejects the repression of a materialist society and delves deeply into the darker secrets of nature—in the swamp.

If you are a witch practicing under one of those rays, knowing when that ray is active, it will intensify your magic. Of course, you can double the power when they are active for your spells no matter which branch you fall under.

APPENDIX F

Tarot Card Meanings

Below are some of the meanings for the tarot cards mentioned in this book.

Card	Meanings
Fool	Innocent, curious, spontaneous, carefree, leap of faith, naïve
Magician	Has all the tools of transformation, manifestation, connection between heaven and earth/conscious and subconscious
High Priestess	Inner knowledge, inner wisdom, holder/revealer of sacred secrets behind the veil
Empress	Mother archetype, creativity, nurturing, sensuality, bringing something into being
Emperor	Father figure, setting structure, boundaries, ruler, clear right or wrong
Hierophant	Organized/traditional religion, teacher, share the rules of spirituality, principles, values
Lovers	Garden of Eden, follow temptation or choose a harder path for greater good, romantic involvement
Chariot	Focus, discipline, determination, strength, make decision and follow through
Strength	Inner strength, subtle control/power, instinctual power
Hermit	Introspection, spiritual journey, soul searching
Wheel/Fortune	Karmic cycles, change is coming, stay flexible, a turning point, up becomes down and vice versa

Card	Meanings
Justice	Universal Law, balance, truth revealed
Hanged Man	New perspective, look around, compromise, waiting for more information/enlightenment
Death	Natural endings and beginnings, letting go, finalize to move on, end of a cycle
Temperance	Balance, harmony integrating, blending of opposites, promise
Devil	Temptation to take the easy way out, addictions
Tower	Sudden ending of old structures
Star	Drawing from the waters of consciousness, hope springs eternal, highly spiritual
Moon	Secrets, let quiet times heal you
Sun	Rejoice, enjoy the ride, celebration
Judgment	A calling, be lifted, respond, rise up
World	Completion of one cycle/phase and the beginning of another, taking the good with you.

ACKNOWLEDGMENTS

People often think a person writes a book alone, but authors know it takes a village of friends, lovers, and supporters to get through the gauntlet of writing a book. I want to thank my beautiful team for their unending support: Marlene Morris, the center of my love and inspiration; Lisa Hagan, my agent and cherished friend; Kate Zimmermann, my talented and patient editor; Raven Keyes, my amazing bright light of joy and wisdom; Jackie Zeman, my darling friend and encourager; Aurora Heinemann, for anointing me a Mystic; Heidi Hening, another bright and shining light in my life; Anam Cara Cat, a true enlightened being of love; Hercules Invictus, who inspires people every day of his life; Don Burgess, who always holds the light high to illuminate the way; Donna Nicholson, for being a Reiki light; Kat Neff, one of the world's most amazing people; Brenda Knight, an inspired Muse; Obi-Ron Schultz, a man of many talents; Shelley Kaehr, a brilliant woman of this world and the next; Victor Fuhrman, for his open heart and wonderful friendship; Pamela and Ralph Ventura, who bring light into every life they touch; and to Sr. Ruth Marie Gibbons, for being the first person to believe in my gifts. I thank them from the depths of my being. Without you all, I might be just a dreamer and not a doer.

Love love, love,
kac

IMAGE CREDITS

Courtesy of Artvee: 123

Caroline Casey: 42, 162

Courtesy of Dover: 211

Getty Images: *DigitalVision Vectors:* clu: 87; duncan1890: 74, 120; ilbusca: 127; PaCondryx: 39, 138; Renphoto: 10; *E+:* Andrew_Howe: 21; *iStock/Getty Images Plus:* arxichtu4ki: 187; Benjavisa: 81; Bitter: 26; ChrisGorgio: 35; denisk0: 118; L Feddes: 117; ma_rish: 100; Zdenek Sasek: 147; Inna Sinano: 97 (right), 153 (left)

Courtesy of Getty Museum: 154

Courtesy of New York Public Library: 60

Courtesy of Rawpixel: 53, 59, 64, 84, 91, 96, 97 (left), 99, 106, 128, 131, 132, 145, 150, 171, 174

Shutterstock.com: Amber_Sun: 77; Kovalov Anatolii: cover, throughout (rainbow); annamyslivets: 68; artellia: 33; Aysel Badalova: 202; Victoria Bat: cover, throughout (orbit, frame, stars); carlos 401: 124; Cat_arch_angel: 67; Anasteisha Fox: 14; Alena Ganzhela: 73; Gringoann.art: 102; Daria Karpova: 149; Anastasia Lembrik: 16; Marta Leo: 23; littlewhiterat: 175; John Lock: 58; moibalkon: 135; oixxo: 141; patrimonio designs ltd: 83; BOONCHUAY PROMJIAM: 47; Reline Vector: 8; Sidhe: 105; Alena Solonshchikova: 51, 56, 90, 114, 121, 161, 164, 165; Sonya illustration: 4, 5; Bodor Tivadar: 55; Valedi: 25; WinWin artlab: 5 (triangle moon); Wonder-studio: 19; Valeriya Yanchkovskaya: 142; Yudina Anna: 66; uladzimir zgurski: 194, 195; Katya Zlobina: 157, 159; Zoart Studio: 202

INDEX

ABOUT THE AUTHOR

Kac Young has been a producer, writer, and director in the Hollywood television industry for over twenty-five years. She has earned PhDs in natural health, naturopathy, and clinical hypnotherapy and completed thirty-six courses in nutrition from Baylor University. She is the author of twenty-seven books, including *Essential Oils for Beginners, The Quick Guide to Bach Flower Remedies, Crystal Power, Living the Faery Life,* and *Magical Trees,* as well as Llewellyn's *Essential Oils Calendar* for 2020, 2021, and 2022. She also has a monthly podcast called *The Art of Healing.*

Kac's entertainment credits include *General Hospital, Showtime Comedy Club Network, Politically Incorrect, Circus of the Stars, The People's Choice Awards, The Golden Globe Awards, The Genesis Awards,* and several dozen specials with Hollywood's biggest stars. She has served on the boards of the Directors Guild of America and Women in Film, and has won multiple awards, including an Iris Award for her work as a producer of *Mama* and a Golden Acorn Award for *Cleaning Up Your Act.* Most recently, Kac was vice president of television production and development for Universal Studios Hollywood.

Kac is also a licensed religious science minister, a certified archetypal therapist and counselor, a certified meditation teacher, a certified medical qigong instructor, a master feng shui practitioner, a career coach for aspiring actors and directors, and a former pilot of private airplanes. She teaches classes in crystal healing, essential oils, feng shui, meditation, pendulum therapy, and qigong. Clients come to her for advice on physical, mental, and spiritual well-being. She actively fights for animal rights, and to foster and preserve women's rights.

Find her online at kacyoung.com.